PRIMAF

PROFESSIONAL BOO

NICHOLAS BIELBY

© 1994 Nicholas Bielby
34567890 90123

Published by Scholastic Publications Ltd
Villiers House
Clarendon Avenue
Leamington Spa
Warwickshire CV32 5PR

Author Nicholas Bielby
Editor Noel Pritchard
Assistant Editor Kate Banham
Series Designer Lynne Joesbury

This book is written for Jessica Marion Cartington Howey who is only just beginning to talk, never mind read.

Designed using Aldus Pagemaker
Processed by Pages Bureau, Leamington Spa

British Library Cataloguing-in-Publication Data
A catalogue record for this book is available from the British Library.

ISBN 0-590-53305-3

PRIMARY
PROFESSIONAL BOOKSHELF

CONTENTS

PRIMARY

PROFESSIONAL BOOKSHELF

PRIMARY
PROFESSIONAL BOOKSHELF

INTRODUCTION

THE AIM OF THIS BOOK

This book is intended for teachers and student teachers who want to understand more about how children learn to read. It seeks to present an account, based on up-to-date research, of the developing processes by which children learn to read, and its aim is to provide teachers with a theory to underpin their practice.

Reading is the process of making sense of messages that have been encoded in writing. Making sense of such messages involves both decoding and comprehending text. This book will consider what is involved in both these processes. The approach taken traces the reading process from the black marks on the page to comprehension; and it also traces development from pre-reading skills, through various stages and strategies to skilled, adult reading processes.

The argument of this book is that, under adult guidance and instruction, children teach themselves to read. Since their knowledge of language when they first come to reading is knowledge of *spoken* language, learning to read is initially a matter of relating written language to this existing knowledge.

At the same time, of course, the written code of English is alphabetic. Thus, the written forms of words in English represent the *sounds* of the spoken words. Learning to read inevitably involves processes of translating written language into the more familiar spoken language forms. This coming together of an alphabetic script with existing spoken language knowledge determines the nature of the learning process. The task is learning to relate spellings with known pronunciations.

PHONOLOGICAL PROCESSES

The reading process develops through many stages. The first stage involves children recognising and naming whole words ('It says "Ford"!') in much the same kind of way that they might recognise cars ('It's an Escort!'). The next stage involves the alphabetic principle that letters and combinations of letters represent the sounds in known spoken words. The ultimate stage is the one where word-meanings are identified directly, and virtually instantaneously, from their spellings. A major theme of this book is the way in which the child's knowledge of spoken language and the sounds of spoken language are employed at every stage and in every aspect of reading development.

There are many relevant aspects of the child's knowledge of spoken language to consider – for example, comprehension of written language correlates closely with comprehension of spoken language. But perhaps most immediately significant for our purposes are the ways sound patterns represent meanings. The theory of the ways in which sounds systematically encode meanings is called phonology. The term 'phonological' is going to be central to the argument in this book, so let us look at the meaning of this term.

At its simplest, it is a phonological process that enables us to distinguish between the words 'come' and 'gum' when we hear them. We hear the difference so clearly, and their meanings are so distinct, that we have probably never thought how close the sounds of the two words are to each other. Try saying the words aloud and notice how you make the different sounds. For the two sounds /k/ and /g/, the physical acts involved in producing them are very similar. If you touch your voice box or hold your hand in front of your mouth while saying them, you will notice some of the differences. Fortunately, however, for our purposes we don't need to know about how different sounds are produced. The study of such differences is phonetics, not phonology. We are concerned with hearing the individual sounds that are significant for distinguishing one word from another.

In phonology, we are concerned with the significant sounds a language uses to encode meanings. And these sounds are paralleled, albeit imperfectly, in the spellings of written language. Learning to read involves mapping phonological patterns on to orthographic (spelling) patterns.

Many aspects of phonology are significant in the reading process. Hearing rhymes is one such aspect, as are the skills of segmentation which enable us to decide how many distinct sounds (phonemes) there are in a word such as 'ox' (more than there are letters!). Short-term auditory memory is another aspect – for example, the ability that enables us to remember a telephone number as we rehearse it to ourselves while we press the buttons. It is a 'phonological process' that enables us, in silent reading, to 'hear' what we read in our mind's ear. Reading by phonics is another phonological process – or rather, a bundle of phonological processes!

CHANGING APPROACHES AND CURRENT THEORY

Recognition of the crucial role of phonological processes in reading development has come about, surprisingly, only fairly recently. As far as academic research is concerned, it has come into prominence only in the last 15 years or so and, as far as reading schemes are concerned, it only began to appear in the new schemes of 1994.

The new ideas relating to phonological processes are not to be confused with the traditional teaching of phonics. Indeed, traditional phonics teaching needs to be reassessed in the light of the findings about phonological processes. The term 'the new phonics' in the title of this book is used deliberately to contrast with traditional phonics. But further, the term 'phonics' itself should be understood not as referring to a teaching method, but rather, as Ken Goodman (1993) insists, to the complex relationships between the sound system and the spelling system of language. To avoid confusion about the term 'phonics', we shall generally use the term 'graphophonics' to refer to the relationship between the written and sound systems. How we can most usefully help children to understand these relationships depends on the development of the child's phonological skills.

The child comes to the task of learning to read equipped with:

+ her knowledge of spoken language;
+ her desire to communicate and to please;
+ her creative intelligence and desire to understand;
+ her experience of living in a literate world;
+ her visual processing system.

The child's job is to make sense of both the written texts and the teaching she is presented with. The teacher's job is to match the learning experiences and instruction she provides to the child's current skills and learning processes. This means, for the teacher, not simply following, but anticipating and leading the child's spontaneous learning processes. In order to be able to do this, the teacher must have an idea of the strategies and skills the child is currently employing, and a theoretical perspective on the directions in which development should be progressing.

In general, the theory this book presents is an information-processing theory. It is about the way in which, when we look at print, we process the information we take in through our eyes and relate it to what we already know (including spoken language) in order to make sense of it. In this way, the theory is in the mainstream of contemporary cognitive psychology.

However, this book isn't just a textbook about the psychology of reading. Hopefully, the way the theory is presented will highlight its relevance to the teacher. As the theory unfolds, so does the discussion of its implications for teaching. The book starts with a discussion of theoretical perspectives and ends with a discussion of the teacher's task.

HOW IS THIS BOOK ORGANISED?

Chapter 1, 'The need for theory', starts with a discussion of the contemporary debate about methods of teaching reading, distinguishing between approaches that emphasise the decoding of print and approaches that emphasise the construction of meanings. It goes on to discuss our implicit theories and argues the need for a clear, explicit theory which will help us find our bearings. Contemporary research suggests a theory that marries decoding approaches with approaches that emphasise meaning. Such a theory can help us understand the processes of learning to read so that we can help children in more effective ways.

Chapter 2, 'Interaction in theory and practice', develops the context of ideas broached in the first chapter. First, it elaborates on the distinction between 'top-down' processes of using existing knowledge to infer meanings and 'bottom-up' processes of decoding print into words, and argues that both are necessary for effective reading. Secondly, it discusses the ways children learn by constructing their own theories and concepts – these are the skills of learning they bring with them to the task of learning to read. Thirdly, it examines everyday hiccups and errors in adult reading in order to highlight the complexity of interacting processes at work. Again, this highlights the need for a theoretical overview for understanding the processes involved.

In Chapter 3, 'Modelling the reading process', theory is tackled head on. An information-processing model of reading is discussed that explains the relative contributions of the bottom-up processing of print and the top-down application of existing knowledge to the production of meaning from a text. The bottom-up contribution involves the combination of phonological skills derived from spoken language with the visual skills of perceiving patterns in print. The top-down processes involve the contribution of experience both of life and of language patterns to reconstructing the meaning of a text.

Chapter 4, 'Developmental stages in learning to read', discusses the phases and processes of reading development – both the surface characteristics of children's reading behaviour, and the underlying systems and strategies that are developing. It traces the development of reading skills through the pre-reading and the sight-vocabulary (logographic) stage, when children recognise whole words they have previously learned, to the 'phonological recoding' (alphabetic) stage in which print-words are translated (or 'recoded') into sound-words that the child can then recognise. The skills of attending to all the letters of the word in sequence finally lead the child into the orthographic stage where meaning is derived more directly and automatically from the spellings of words. In following this development, the chapter traces the importance of spelling skills in facilitating reading skills.

The following two chapters explore in more detail the two bottom-up processes. Chapter 5, 'Phonological processing', examines the crucial role of phonological processes in providing the child with a 'self-teaching mechanism', together with its contribution to the development of orthographic processing. Chapter 6, 'Orthographic processing', explores the processes of the visual identification of words from their spellings. In particular, the emphasis falls on the processes of learning to recognise regular spelling sequences instantly as they appear in different words, and the establishment of a fully-processed sight vocabulary.

In Chapters 7 and 8, 'The quest for meaning: context and syntax' and 'The quest for meaning: semantics and comprehension', the drive to make sense is considered. All the many aspects of 'context' (grammar, semantics, general knowledge, and so on) are discussed in relation to their contribution to making sense of the text. The chapters consider how children use their existing knowledge to help make sense of texts, both in terms of 'reading the lines' and 'reading between the lines'.

The last two chapters are concerned with 'putting it all together' in relation to classroom practice. Chapter 9, 'Putting it together: children's reading strategies', looks at the ways children use the skills and experience they possess when tackling a reading task, and the ways we, as teachers, can assess and interpret their strategies. Each child has a developing repertoire of strategies, and the teacher needs to learn diagnostic skills in order to understand how the child is tackling the reading task. In the final chapter, 'Putting it together: the teacher's task', the role of the teacher is discussed. The teacher needs to put theory and practical experience together in arriving at an understanding of how to help the child at the particular stage she has reached, whether she requires instruction or simply prompting, practice and encouragement. The teacher's aim should be to work smoothly with the grain of the child's spontaneous development, guiding and leading it towards effective, skilled reading.

I should like to take this opportunity of recording my gratitude to Gina Nuttall and Noel Pritchard of Scholastic and Roger Beard of Leeds University for their generous encouragement and support, and to my student, Vicki Preece, for advising me about intelligibility. Any gaucheries and solecisms remaining in the text are all my own. I should also point out the convention of putting words and letters between slashes (for example, /m/) is a means of referring to the sound and not the spelling involved.

CHAPTER 1

THE NEED FOR THEORY

The current debate about methods of teaching reading results from conflicting theories about the reading process. What we might call the traditional view is that children first need to learn the code of black marks on the page by processes of rote learning, and only then can they put them together into words and sentences and meaningful messages. In fact, this view underpins at least three traditional theories: the classic 'alphabetic' method (see-ay-tee spells 'cat'); the phonic method of teaching reading by 'sounding-out' routines; and 'look-and-say' methods of whole-word teaching (for example, using flashcards). One way or another, the traditional view is that we need to identify words before we can go on to construct meaning from them.

The alternative view that has dominated approaches to the teaching of reading for 15 years or so emphasises meaning and the use of meaning as the *means* of identifying words. This is done by using the context and one's experience of language to guide intelligent guessing, using minimal information from the printed text. Thus, at the beginning of a story, if the first word is 'Once', it is a fair guess that the next words will be either 'upon a time' or 'there was a...'. The reader looks at the text to check her guess.

The traditional approach of building up the words from the letters is (often disparagingly) called 'decoding', and the meaning-orientated approach is called the 'whole language' or 'language experience' approach. These approaches are distinguished by their views on what has priority in the reading process. Traditional views emphasise the process of building up towards meaning from the visual information on the page, and so these processes are known as 'bottom-up' processes. The language-experience approach emphasises the role of the higher mental processes and the use of the context of meanings to give clues about what the words should be saying. Such processes are called 'top-down' processes. Bottom-up approaches emphasise controlled vocabulary, designed to facilitate decoding procedures while top-down approaches emphasise quality of story and naturalness of language to motivate and facilitate anticipation of meanings and words. In the former view, then, identifying the words precedes constructing the meaning; in the latter, the ongoing construction of meaning predicts the word to come.

Of the four books on the teaching of reading that are, according to Greg Brooks *et al.* (1992), most widely recommended to students, three are very clearly in the top-down camp. These books are Liz Waterland's *Read With Me* (1985), Margaret Meek's *Learning to Read* (1982) and Frank Smith's *Reading* (1978, 1985). Their approach is typically associated with the debate about reading with 'real books'. But, in point of fact, their top-down approach underpins virtually every reading scheme currently in use.

This top-down approach is now being called into question from two quarters. Firstly, what we might call the 'back to basics' brigade is challenging it in the name of 'standards'. The call to traditional values includes the call to 'traditional' approaches to teaching reading. But there is also a more academically respectable view emerging, as a result of reading research, in favour of bottom-up approaches. This maintains that bottom-up processes, underpinned by the child's 'phonological awareness' of the constituent sounds within words, have a much greater part to play than is generally acknowledged by language-experience theorists. These new theoretical ideas have informed some new reading schemes and the revisions to the National Curriculum for English. As it happens, of course, teachers in the classroom never lost sight of the importance of bottom-up processing – they were just made to feel guilty about it.

What this book is aiming to do, in terms of theory, is to present a model of the reading process that rescues what is good and important from both traditional and language-experience approaches, and show how they can be reconciled in a wider theory based in contemporary reading research. The intention, then, is to:

✦ show how the marriage of top-down and bottom-up processes is vital to reading success;

✦ provide a model of the development of reading processes;

✦ show the crucial role of phonological processes in the child's development of reading strategies;

✦ indicate the ways in which the teacher can promote and facilitate the development of reading processes.

PHONICS AND THE 'NEW PHONICS'

We have already touched on the issue of phonics and the 'new phonics'. But, since there is a danger that any challenge to the existing language-experience orthodoxy in the name of bottom-up processing will be viewed as a call to return to traditional phonics, it is important to deal with this issue very explicitly.

For nearly two decades the theoretical running has been made by the language-experience approach. Frank Smith's (1978, 1985) phrase about children 'learning to read by reading' has become a slogan for this theoretical viewpoint, but recently phonics has started to make something of a comeback. Peter Bryant (1993) argues that:

> There is no doubt at all that the work of experimental psychologists over the last decade has, by and large, provided us with a convincing rationale for 'phonics' teaching. (page 89)

But he is not advocating traditional 'phonics first and fast', the approach that argues that phonics and phonic word-building make up the first step to be taught in reading. He is not advocating that we teach reading *by* phonics so much as teach phonics *within* reading. Research has shown that some of the skills involved in phonic sounding-out routines only develop as a *result* of beginning to write and read. Such skills cannot be exploited as the starting-point.

The 'new phonics' is distinguished from traditional phonics teaching by the following characteristics:

◆ It is, in the first place, a theory about reading, not a method of teaching reading.

◆ It is based on a considerable body of recent research about how children learn and teach themselves.

◆ It emphasises the role of phonological processing at *all* stages of reading development.

◆ Its practical classroom suggestions and implications are underpinned by the research.

There are ways, of course, in which it is like traditional phonics. Its approach is essentially bottom-up rather than top-down. That is, it is concerned with *deriving* meaning from the print on the page, rather than *ascribing* meaning to print by guessing what it is likely to say. It recognises that printed texts are messages written in code. The code consists of black marks on the page, and we need to learn how to decode those black marks in order to get at the messages.

The 'new phonics', then, is a bottom-up theory about decoding print. But, since it is also concerned with the whole range of phonological processes involved in reading, it follows the process further upwards than simply identifying words from print. For example, phonological processes are also involved in remembering and making sense of phrases and sentences.

MAKING SENSE OF PRINT

The purpose of reading is to gain meaning from texts. Although this book is largely concerned with bottom-up processes, the aim of looking at these processes is to understand better how we derive meaning from texts. Learning to read is not simply a passive application of decoding rules and routines, but a process of children using *all* their language knowledge, literacy experience and decoding skills to solve the problem of print. In doing this, *children construct their own reading processes*, and these processes include working on the code as well as working on the context. Most children will learn to read whatever method of teaching we employ. This is because to a great degree what they learn is both more than, and different from, what we teach them. It would be nice if they could learn what they need to learn independently of, or even despite, our teaching! But sadly, this isn't generally the case.

Nevertheless, Margaret Clark (1976) showed that 'there are children... who can learn to read without formal instruction' (page 105). She goes on to argue that 'any theory of reading is adequate only in so far as it takes account of children such as these' (page 106). The theory which will be presented in this book claims, among other things, to show how phonological processing acts as a self-teaching mechanism, helping children invent strategies to try to crack the code for themselves.

If children are doing all this meaning-making for themselves, what is the teacher's role? Is it simply to provide the stimulus, support and encouragement to make sure that children want to try to crack the code for themselves? You might suspect that this is the entire role of the teacher as far as Liz Waterland's 'apprenticeship' and other 'real books' approaches are concerned. Margaret Meek (1982) even suggests that teachers have made themselves unnecessary. And Frank Smith (1988) argues that the role of the teacher is simply promotional, encouraging children to 'join the literacy club'!

However, there is more to it than this. As Marie Clay (1991) points out, it is not certain that children will teach themselves effective strategies. What they invent may be wrong or misleading, and may not be helpful for further development. The teacher should have a clear idea about whether or not the child's strategies are going to be useful in the long run, and intervene to promote and develop useful strategies and to divert children from unproductive ones. To be able to do this, the teacher must have a theoretic approach to the processes of learning to read. She needs a model of the complex and changing processes of reading development in order to be able to teach effectively 'with the grain' of spontaneous development.

TOP-DOWN AND BOTTOM-UP PROCESSING

Since the concepts of top-down and bottom-up processing are so central to the argument of this book, we need to enlarge upon the distinction that we have drawn above. Jeanne Chall (1983) defines the distinction thus:

> The top-down models relate... to the meaning-emphasis approaches of beginning reading and stress the first importance of language and meaning for reading comprehension and also for word recognition... The reader theoretically samples the text in order to confirm and modify initial hypotheses.

> The bottom-up models – those that view the reading process as developing from perception of letters, spelling patterns, and words, to sentence and paragraph meaning, resemble the code-emphasis, beginning reading approaches. (pages 28–9)

Top-down approaches emphasise the knowledge and experience of language and life that the child brings to the text. For Kenneth Goodman (1967), reading is 'a psycholinguistic guessing game' in which the child predicts or guesses (he uses both terms) the next word. In this 'guessing-game', the child uses various contextual 'cues' (or clues) derived from the preceding text, both from its grammar and its meaning.

One of the clearest signs that there is something in this argument is that children, when they 'miscue' and substitute one word for another, rarely put in words that do not fit grammatically. For example, Samantha (Year 1), reading from a *Link-up* reading scheme book, says, '...at the paper shoe,' for '...at the paper shop'. Clearly she is using visual cues (the first three letters), and equally clearly she is *not* using meaning cues (it doesn't make sense!). What she *has* done is substitute a noun for a noun where a noun is needed.

The top-down Goodman model of the reading process proceeds through these steps:

✦ Sampling: choosing cues from the visible text to provide the minimum amount of information necessary to get effectively to a meaning. The sampled cues serve as a basis for prediction.

✦ Predicting: anticipating meaning, using the meaning of the text so far, and the grammar, to predict what word is coming next.

✦ Confirming: monitoring progress, checking to see if predictions are confirmed by the text and if the reading makes sense.

✦ Correcting: when mismatches between predictions and cues are spotted, or the reading appears inconsistent and not to be making sense, correction strategies involving going back and resampling the text are brought into play.

The concept of sampling and checking against the text begs the question: how is this done except by processing the print? It suggests an interaction between top-down and bottom-up processes. But it also begs the further question: if you can process the print for purposes of sampling and checking, why not for full word identification in the first place? Goodman's answer to this is couched in terms of economy of effort and efficiency. For example, he says:

> Efficiency requires that (the child) sample just enough of the
> phonic information to make predictions and inferences, as
> well as confirm her prior expectations of the text.
> (Goodman 1993, page 60)

Bottom-up theory, however, tends to question this notion of efficiency. Experimental studies have suggested that skilled readers find it more economical and efficient to read all the text using lower level decoding processes, rather than use higher level comprehension processes for guessing and checking. Higher level processing capacity is better used for *making sense* of the whole text, rather than *making up* the text. Marilyn Jager Adams (1990) concludes:

> When reading for comprehension, skilled readers tend to
> look at each individual word and to process its component
> letters quite thoroughly. (page 102)

Further, Goodman's account doesn't explain where the language context comes from initially, if not from words you have already identified. Linnea Ehri (1991) argues that you need to be able to sight-read more than 80 per cent of a text before you have sufficient context to be able to guess tolerably accurately. Jesse Reid (1993) argues that in continuous reading, with only the linguistic context preceding the word to be guessed to go on, success rates even with university students are at best in the order of 27 per cent. And the reader is clearly not in a good position to guess words that come early in a passage or sentence, where no context has yet been established. There are many reasons for questioning Goodman's notion of efficiency.

In contrast with Goodman, for whom 'prediction' is of the essence, Harris and Coltheart (1986) maintain that language is 'essentially unpredictable' (page 170). They go on to claim that research suggests that when words are identified in reading 'context appears to influence word identification only *after* a word has been identified' (page 171).

On the face of it, this sounds paradoxical. But their argument is that after a word has been identified from its letters, it is then checked for sense in context. The effect of context is, they suggest, not to *facilitate* word identification in the first place (as Goodman claims), but to *check out* whether the word identified makes sense. Instead of top-down processing predicting a word, and then bottom-up processing checking to see if it looks correct, it seems as if bottom-up processing identifies a word from the spelling, and then top-down processing checks it for meaning.

Harris and Colheart's is a different version of top-down/bottom-up interaction from the one implicit in Goodman's thesis. What is clear, however, is that, both for Goodman and for Harris and Coltheart, interactive cross-checking between top-down and bottom-up processes takes place.

Chall (1983), in discussing top-down and bottom-up processes, identifies a third group of psychological process models – the 'interactive' models of reading that involve both of these processes. She goes on to state that all these models propose:

> In reading, the reader at some point uses three types of information about a word: grapho-phonemic, semantic and syntactic. (page 29)

That is to say, grammar (syntax), meaning (semantics) and letter–sound (grapho-phonemic) relationships are all seen to be involved in reading. If grammar and meaning involve top-down processes and letter–sound relationships bottom-up, any adequate account of the reading process is going to postulate top-down/bottom-up interaction.

Chall is a major proponent of bottom-up phonics teaching. On the other hand, Ken Goodman is a major proponent of top-down approaches to teaching. Yet he has arrived at similar conclusions to Chall:

> I... learned that readers have not just one but three systems of information to bring to any text – graphophonic, syntactic and semantic – and that each one supports the other two. In the course of making sense of print, we use all three systems, and in using them we learn them. (1993, page 53)

Nevertheless, in addition to their different prioritisation of processes and their consequent difference in approach to teaching, there is another significant difference between Chall and Goodman. Chall's term 'grapho-phonemic' refers to phonemes, the smallest sound units in speech, and how they are represented in writing. Typically, processes depending on such relationships will involve the traditional phonic procedures of sounding out the letters and then blending the sounds. Goodman's term 'graphophonic' refers to a wider range of possible relationships between spellings and sounds. These include processing spelling in 'chunks' and whole-word spelling–sound relationships. For example, if a child recognises that '–ation' always says /ayshun/, or can read the name 'Dwight' because it must rhyme with 'light', she is using graphophonic, not grapho-phonemic processes. The broader meaning of the term 'graphophonic' will prove the more useful to us as the argument of this book develops.

While, then, there remain differences between bottom-up and top-down theorists as to which process makes the running and which is a check on the other, there is common ground. Most significantly, they agree that three sources of information come together in making sense of a text: graphophonic, semantic and syntactic information.

CURRENT TEACHING THEORIES IN SCHOOLS

HMI (1990) reported that:

> There is no evidence of teachers and schools rushing into a single method of teaching reading. The great majority of teachers, almost 85 per cent, used a blend of methods to teach initial reading skills. In less than 18 per cent of cases was a single method – phonics, look and say, or 'real books' – used exclusively or even predominantly. There is clear evidence that adherence to a single approach, whatever the particular method, hindered the children's reading development...

The approach commonly taken in schools seems to be echoed in teacher training. On the subject of approaches to teaching reading, Greg Brooks *et al.* (1992) observe that 'eclecticism rules' (page 30).

But, as Brooks goes on to show, in teacher training, top-down 'meaning-centred' approaches are favoured at the expense of traditional bottom-up 'code-centred' approaches. About 60 per cent of students said they were taught little or nothing about phonics, with fewer than 35 per cent of students reporting that they had been taught about phonics teaching. On the other hand, all courses, according to their staff, featured phonics. Staff claimed to view phonics as indispensable, though inadequate on its own. There was a tendency, however, to belittle 'code-centred' approaches like phonics even while discussing them.

Of the four most widely recommended books on reading, only one is not firmly in the 'meaning-centred' camp and expressly hostile to 'code-centred' approaches including phonics, and this book (Roger Beard's *Developing Reading 3–13* [1987]) is eclectic in its approach.

The reading scheme that stood out as the most highly recommended, *Story Chest*, is, in its Teacher's File (1993), distinctly lukewarm about phonics and dismisses it as 'mere decoding'. 'Code-centred' approaches seem to be discouraged. While 'eclecticism rules' in teacher training, then, it's a somewhat biased form of eclecticism!

It is impressive, considering the climate in training in the recent past, that so many teachers still teach phonics as part of their eclectic approach. Perhaps on a day-to-day basis they continually rediscover that children respond to 'code-centred' as well as 'meaning-centred' teaching approaches. They are responding to what they discover works. In fact, they are responding to the learning strategies that children spontaneously latch on to and develop for themselves.

OUR IMPLICIT THEORIES

Student teachers tend to complain that they aren't told enough about how to teach children to read. Even experienced early years teachers feel a bit insecure about the teaching of reading. They are made to feel guilty that they aren't doing enough, and that they aren't doing it right. They probably feel that they didn't learn enough in training to know what they should be doing; and that what they learned in training doesn't quite tally with what their experience has subsequently taught them. They are made to feel guilty about using schemes, about 'real books', about doing phonics and about *not* doing phonics. What they feel most frustrated by is that they have been given no clear model of how reading works nor of the processes of learning to read.

Of course, we all have theories of some kind about teaching reading, even if these theories are more implicit than explicit.

Helen Arnold (1985) reminds us that the 'ploys' teachers use in helping children to read aloud are patterned by their underlying perceptions of reading. We can perhaps unearth our 'underlying perceptions' (or implicit theories) by examining the teaching strategies (a kinder expression than 'ploys'!) most commonly used to help a child who is stuck on a word. The following are some possible strategies we might find ourselves using, with comments about the implicit theories that seem to go with them.

1. We immediately tell the child the right word.
We do this to keep up the momentum of the reading because we believe in the flow of the story. We hope that next time the child will recognise the word as a sight-vocabulary word — though the chances of this actually happening, if the child hasn't really worked at looking at and analysing the word, are fairly minimal!

2. We wait, giving the child time to work it out.
We believe that reading is a problem-solving activity and that the child, having worked out the word for herself, will be more likely to know the word again another time. We believe this experience will give her a reinforced confidence in her own capacity to cope with print. We are assuming that the child has strategies for tackling print beyond simple sight-vocabulary recognition.

3. We re-read, or get the child to re-read, the sentence fluently up to the problem word, and then leave a question mark dangling.
We expect the child to be able to use the context of meaning to anticipate (or guess) what word ought to come next. This approach regards the child's construction of meaning as crucial and tends to place less emphasis on studying the problem word itself for clues than on building up a sense of where the meaning is going.

4. We point to the first letter and ask the child, 'What does the first letter say?'

This is a minimal phonic approach, avoiding many of the problems that come with phonics, like variable vowels (for example, *a* in *as*, *was*, *saw*), digraphs (for example, *th*, *ea*), the silent 'e' rule, irregular spellings, auditory memory and the blending of sounds. It tends, however, to encourage habits of inattention to the spelling of the whole word and cannot, in itself, be a complete strategy for the child since more than one word begins with any given sound! Using it, we assume that the child will be employing context cues for herself.

5. We combine strategies 3 and 4.

This is the strategy we tend most commonly to use. We are assuming that the initial sound suggests a short list of candidate words. When we re-read the sentence, we are assuming that the context of both grammar and meaning is going to suggest candidate words. We invite the child to sound the initial letter and guess in the hope that there is just one word that satisfies both the sound and context criteria. This approach, then, combines the top-down use of context cues and the bottom-up decoding of the black marks on the page. It is a strategy that children tend to pick up early and employ for themselves. It overcomes an immediate problem, but doesn't seem to do much for progress because it isn't a reliable strategy for word identification except in *very* predictable texts.

6. We ask the child to sound out all the letters in sequence and then blend the sounds.

This strategy is, of course, traditional phonics – the stereotypical 'code-centred' approach. The theory is based on the fact that our written script is alphabetic: that is, that the basic symbols don't stand for words, syllables or meanings, but for the minimal units of sound that distinguish one word from another. Unfortunately for the theory of phonics, and for children, the correspondence between letters and phonemes (these minimal units of sound) is not reliable. Nevertheless, in controlled situations, sounding out the letters can work fairly reliably. Such controlled situations, where irregularities of spelling are avoided and vowels are limited to only one of their possible sounds, tend to be very restricted situations in which meaning and naturalness are sacrificed for the sake of regularity of spelling. For example:

> My cat can be Tab. Tab can have ham and jam in a pan.
>
> (Garfield, 1992)

There are yet further problems with phonics, but phonic strategies certainly have their place in the repertoire. At least they make the child study all the letters in the word in their sequence.

7. We cover part of the word, leaving a simple constituent part of the word visible, hoping the child will be able to read it.

At its simplest this strategy may involve covering up the final inflection on a word and displaying the stem, for example, if the problem word is 'talked', covering the '-ed' and leaving the word 'talk' to be identified. We are assuming the child has a sight vocabulary that this process can tap into. Not only can such an approach give the child confidence that she knows something, but it also demonstrates a strategy of analysing the word into known chunks that will later come to have many uses. However, there can be problems – you would not show the child the known chunk 'not' if the problem word were 'nothing'!

8. We prompt the child to explore the illustrations for clues to meaning.

With early readers and their limited vocabulary, the story is often told *between* the words and pictures. It is quite likely that the teacher will already have held a warm-up discussion of the book and the illustrations with the child before reading begins in order to establish a context of relevant meanings. In drawing attention to the picture, the teacher is prompting a relevant guess. If the child learns that a guess prompted by things other than the printed word gets credit, maybe this is not such a good thing to learn. Poor readers are often characterised by wandering eyes that do not study the text, and by using guesses to compensate for weak decoding skills.

9. We remind the child of previous encounters with the problem word.

It is often the case that children will fail to read a word they have previously read successfully. Or the situation may be that the child was told the word on a previous page. If the child turns back and finds the previous place, this often proves effective, as if the visual context were an effective prompt. Children also tend to have an idea of which words are *their* words that they know and take responsibility for. Anticipatory prompts from the teacher like, 'Do you think you will remember it next time?' could well help, especially if the child has been asked to look at the word analytically.

10. We ask the child prompt questions about the context, hoping this will suggest a plausible guess.

This strategy places meaning in the forefront. On its own, however, such prompts can only stimulate guesses. They depend on the child supplying other more code-centred strategies to complement the contextual ones. Effectively, this is a more diffuse but wider ranging form of strategy 3.

If we use all or most of these strategies from time to time as we think appropriate, we are doing what the vast majority of teachers do. But we tend to use them less for theoretical than for pragmatic reasons: they seem to work. Nevertheless, there are theoretical beliefs underpinning these teacher strategies, even if they are not fully systematised. At their simplest, they include the beliefs that:

+ using meaning-in-context to get at the text is effective;
+ using phonic decoding skills is effective;

✦ simplifying words into known chunks is effective;

✦ combining and prompting different strategies is effective.

As teachers, we spontaneously tend to use a blend of methods and promote a combination of top-down and bottom-up strategies.

SUMMARY

In this chapter we have seen how the debate about reading polarises between an emphasis on top-down processes concerned with contextual meanings and 'prediction', and an emphasis on bottom-up processes concerned with decoding the letters on the page. Yet, since reading involves cross-checking between both these processes, we would be better off looking for an interactive model of reading that takes them both into account. As teachers, our implicit theories are already eclectic, so an explicit, interactive theory should serve to clarify and provide a rationale for our intuitions.

CHAPTER 2

INTERACTION IN THEORY AND PRACTICE

THE AIM OF THIS CHAPTER

In this chapter we will look in greater depth at certain issues raised in the previous chapter. These issues are: the interaction between top-down and bottom-up processes in reading; the way children construct their own reading processes; and the need for a theory to explain the complexities of reading processes as we experience them.

THE MARRIAGE OF TOP-DOWN AND BOTTOM-UP PROCESSING

> Reading is much more than the decoding of black marks upon the page: it is a quest for meaning and one that requires the reader to be an active participant. (Cox Report, 16.2)

Cox is, of course, right: reading is the process of making sense from print in such a way that it largely recovers the meanings and intentions of the writer. His emphasis rightly falls upon the active search for meaning that the reader makes. This search, however, is just as active in decoding as it is in any other part of the enterprise. Making sense goes on at *every* level – and making sense *overall* depends on all the levels working in concert.

Reading is certainly *more* than just decoding the black marks on the page; but it is at least decoding the black marks on the page. The black marks represent the specific wording of the text. The reader's pre-existing language knowledge and experience of the world could not be activated, focused and organised to reconstruct the specific meanings the writer intended without the specific wording on the page being recovered in the first place. This is so obvious that it hardly needs to be said – except that it has been down-played by many influential reading experts following the lead of Ken Goodman and Frank Smith.

Today, however, most experts agree that we have to regard reading as an interactive process – that is, reading depends on the interaction between the bottom-up processing of the black marks on the page and the top-down quest for meaning. Nevertheless, as we have seen, different writers give different accounts of the balance and prioritisation.

Marie Clay (1991), while seeing the reading process as interactive, tends to think that top-down processing has priority. Of all the sources of information that come together in reading, she argues, meaning is the most important:

> It is a source which lies outside the text in the sense that it
> depends upon what the reader is able to bring to the text...
> The reader:
> ✦ brings prior knowledge to the text
> ✦ carries out reading work in order to make sense of what
> he is reading
> ✦ and uses meaning as his ultimate check that all is well.
> (page 292)

Clay seems here to confuse the prior knowledge that we bring *to* the text with the new meaning that we derive *from* the text. It is the text that, through the agency of the reading process, determines the relevant selection of prior knowledge, and how that selection is shaped, modified and elaborated to construct the meaning. Her formulation is misleading, then, in the way it diverts attention from the text as the critical source of information.

Marilyn Jager Adams (1990) seems to reverse Clay's order of priority (and implicitly give the text a more central role). She points out that everything follows from the reader looking at the text:

> When reading, it is visual, orthographic processing that
> comes first and that causes the system to kick in. (page 137)

Yet Clay's and Adams' views are not ultimately in conflict. Indeed, Clay (1972, page 162) herself says that the visual must finally dominate when it comes to determining what the actual words of the text are. It is the visual 'reading work' on the text that starts the whole process going, including the interpretative restructuring of prior knowledge. In line with this, Jessie Reid (1993) maintains that reading is 'interactive with bottom-up priority' (page 29). Bottom-up processes have priority in starting the whole reading system going and in establishing the wording of the text. Top-down processes have priority in determining what the words mean in relation to what the whole text is about. Bottom-up processes identify the words and top-down processes specify their meanings in context. In the overall reading system, these are complementary processes.

A clear theory of how these processes work together in a complementary way should help us to transcend 'mishmash' eclecticism, and to work complementary strategies together in our teaching to support a balanced development of top-down and bottom-up processing in children.

HOW CHILDREN CONSTRUCT THEIR OWN READING PROCESSES

Since we need to match our teaching to those who are learning, we need to take into account how they learn. Our teaching approaches will only fit together and support each other if they fit in with the way children learn to read. In the previous chapter, I said that children construct and develop their own reading processes. The emphasis in contemporary theory falls very much upon the work children do in teaching themselves to read. We can teach children by any method that we like but we cannot determine exactly what sense children will make of it and what they will learn. In fact, they learn a lot more than we teach them – and if they didn't, they really would have problems!

Children teach themselves in many important ways. For example, we can contrast two different strategies for translating (recoding) print into sound-words, traditional phonics and analogy. Children have to be taught the traditional phonic strategies of 'sounding out' the letters in sequence and then blending the sounds; but they are not generally taught to exploit analogies between words they know and new words. Analogy works by inference in this way: if *beak* says /beak/, then a new word, *peak*, should say /peak/, because similar spellings usually rhyme. Children tend to work this out themselves (how they do so will be a major issue in Chapter 5 on phonological processing). They generate their own strategies for making sense of print and, in the face of each word they encounter, they select a strategy for themselves from their repertoire.

Margaret Clark (1976) warns us, 'it is... dangerous to assume... that the way we teach is the way children learn' (page 105). At any particular stage of a child's development, some strategies for making sense of print come more easily and spontaneously than others. Their learning processes are not necessarily attuned to our teaching methods. Rather, being developmental, their learning processes operate according to their own internal logic. What children pay attention to and take from external influences depends on their individual needs and orientations at the time. Their needs are not so individual, however, that there is no general pattern to be observed. Rather, the teacher needs to be alert to the stage of development the child is at and what her needs are. The teaching strategies that will be most useful to children are those that are attuned to the processes that children develop spontaneously. We need to adapt the way we teach to the way children learn.

In trying to do this, we need to bear in mind what active, constructive processes of learning the child brings to the task. We need to remember that the teacher's task is the responsive *leading* of this development towards effective reading strategies. As Marie Clay (1991) says, 'The teaching may have to go the child's way to the teacher's goal' (page 286).

THE CHILD'S WAY OF LEARNING

Learning to read is not peculiar among children's learning activities. Annette Karmiloff-Smith (1984) argues that language acquisition is simply one example of cognitive problem-solving, employing the same processes as all problem-solving. There is, she says, 'a constant motivation for *control*, both over the external environment and over one's own internal representations' (page 40).

Control is achieved through constructing coherent inner representations that are also consistent with external experience.

This 'constructivist' perspective argues that, since learning is a matter of active problem-solving resulting in the reorganisation of mental structures, children essentially teach themselves by developing and correcting their own theories. This applies to reading as much as to anything else: the child is an active, constructive thinker in attempting to make sense of print.

The child progressively tries out various strategies for relating the unknown code of print to the known world of spoken language. This progression of strategies gives rise to the stages of development we will discuss in detail in Chapter 4. A key step comes when the child starts to relate the visual features of print not directly to the *meaning* of the spoken word, but rather to the *sounds* of the spoken word. That is, it comes in the realisation that the code to be cracked is phonological or graphophonic. It is possible for the child to realise this spontaneously, but it is much more likely to be facilitated by deliberate adult demonstration and instruction.

Even though children tend to construct their own strategies in relation to print, there is a role for the teacher. In part, the teacher's role is to instruct children in strategies they won't discover for themselves; in part it is to deflect them from strategies that may be ultimately dysfunctional. For example, children who find the phonological strategies of translating print-words into sound-words problematic may compensate by developing the skill of contextual guessing to a fine art. This tendency to rely on contextual guessing seems to be characteristic of beginning and backward readers, as well as dyslexics. Contextual guessing, as a strategy, does not have much future in it and children who rely too exclusively upon contextual guessing rather than processing the print, tend to experience difficulties in secondary education. This is because new subjects introduce new words and usages, and the texts the children encounter are not as predictable as the texts in primary school. Contextual guessing is a clear example of the kind of situation where a survival strategy children develop to solve an immediate problem, creates greater problems in the long run. The enabling teacher will be alert to such strategies and work at developing approaches with more future mileage in them. These will depend on:

✦ what strategies the child uses/has available;

✦ the value of each strategy for the child's moving on to the next stage of reading development;

✦ methods of promoting and developing the strategies that have most mileage in them for the child's future development.

These requirements imply, of course, that the teacher has a clear model herself of the reading process and the way different elements develop and complement each other. Before, however, we go on to consider this theoretical model of the reading system and how it develops, it will be helpful to examine our subjective adult experience of reading at work to obtain a concrete sense of how the different processes interact in practice.

WHAT WE CAN LEARN FROM READING ERRORS OR 'MISCUES'

In a later chapter we will discuss miscue analysis of children's reading in some detail. Here we will examine our own adult experience of reading, in order to check and relate theory with our own experiences.

When your car's running well you don't need to think about

what goes on under the bonnet. It's only when something goes wrong that you start to learn how the thing works. So it is with adult reading. Mostly, our reading goes smoothly and we don't need to pay attention to the processes that make it work. After all, these processes *are* only being efficient when we don't have to pay them any attention. We need our conscious attention to search for the meaning, but sometimes some minor malfunctions make us aware that there *are* processes going on under the bonnet.

Failures, errors and self-corrections in reading, then, may give us some sort of window into the processes of reading of which we are usually not aware. Even as skilled readers, we all make slips and mistakes in the normal course of reading. If we can make sense of them, we should be in a better position to understand our own reading processes. Here are some examples from my own experience.

EXAMPLE 1

I am tired and I am reading something heavy. I suddenly realise that my eyes have been passing over the words but my mind has been elsewhere. I've been reading on autopilot. My eyes have been moving along the lines and I must have identified some of the words because I can remember some of them, but I have no idea what the book has been saying. So I try re-reading the passage and I deliberately try to pay attention to the words this time, but still it doesn't hang together meaningfully. To concentrate my attention, I read it aloud. Maybe it makes sense this time, or maybe I decide to go and watch television instead.

So what does this show us? There are many levels of processing that need to work in concert, but when you are tired the apparently unitary functioning of these processes breaks down. When you read the passage aloud to yourself to concentrate your attention, you are demonstrating that there are different routes to accessing meaning. The external auditory route is brought into play to support the inner processes, just as counting on your fingers can help with doing sums in your head.

EXAMPLE 2

The translation of print into sound for processing into meaning is a key strategy in learning to read. And even as adults we translate print into sound. My second example touches on this translation even when it is unspoken and only heard inside the head. When reading silently, I have from time to time been annoyed by hearing words mispronounced in my mind's ear. For example, I have read the word 'decade' and have heard it pronounced as if it were spelled 'de*cayed*', not '*deck*-aid'. (The BBC, that bastion of misplaced stresses, almost invariably says 'dec*ade*' these days!) On other occasions I have read 'harassed', and what I have heard in my head is the American-influenced pronunciation, 'har*assed*', when I prefer the traditional English pronunciation '*ha*rassed'.

What does all this go to show? One speculation it suggests is that there may be a link between the assistance that reading aloud can give to comprehension and the 'hearing aloud' that goes on in our heads. But at the moment the main point I want to make is that, even if we don't always pay it much attention, we *do* hear the words we read in our heads, even though it's not immediately obvious why we should.

EXAMPLE 3

I have on a number of occasions been momentarily stumped by the word 'misled'. I have heard it clearly in my head pronounced as if it rhymed with 'drizzled'. And I didn't know what it meant. How could I have been so mizzled?

One thing is certain. I was not reading the word phonically, letter-sound by letter-sound, because it is phonically quite regular. I must, therefore, have been processing the print in some other way. Equally clearly, I was not processing it as a whole word that I knew, matching it against some kind of mental template. I must have been processing the word in some way in chunks bigger than individual letters and smaller than the whole word.

I think that the best explanation is that, because of the

grammar of the sentence, I was anticipating a verb and, in processing a verb, I have an expectation that if it ends with '-ed', I am dealing with a regular past tense, like 'talked' or, even more to the point, like 'drizzled'. Unconsciously, I had divided the word into two parts, thus: *misle + d*. This division is into (a) the first part, that could be called a *stem* (the form of a verb that would make an entry heading in a dictionary) and (b) the last part, the add-on *inflection* that indicates it's in the past tense.

Of course, the correct analysis of 'misled' is *mis + led*. 'Mis' indicates error, as in 'mistake'. 'Led' irregularly incorporates its past-tense status within its form, like 'brought', 'took', 'made' and so on, the so-called 'strong' verbs.

My mistake seems to have been at the level of morphological analysis (dividing the word into its meaningful bits). My mental processing may have dealt with the word in the following fashion:

◆ from the grammatical context, verb anticipated;

◆ from the print on the page, '-ed' identified;

◆ '-ed' fits regular past tense ending expectation;

◆ verb stem identified as *'misle'* (since English spelling does not permit 'misl');

◆ since '-isle' corresponds to no spelling in English that is pronounced with a short 'i', I must have processed 'misle' for sound in two chunks, thus, *'mis + le'*, with *'mis'* working analogously with 'his';

◆ sound-image processed for meaning and draws a blank;

◆ meanwhile, perhaps, the visual recognition processes also draw a blank as a result of faulty morphology;

◆ monitoring for meaning demands reprocessing with a view to self-correction.

One further significant point emerging is that the phonological translation seems to have been on the route to meaning, because it was the erroneous pronunciation that stopped me recognising the word.

So processing is going on at all kinds of levels (syntactic, morphological, phonological), all of which cross-check with each other for 'meaningfulness' at the level of word-recognition, which is the arbiter of whether the processing has been successful. Further, internalised pronunciation seems to be involved in word identification.

EXAMPLE 4

Here is another example involving cross-checking between processes. I recently read the sentence:

> The recent proposals have fairly direct practical implications.

Straightforward enough, you might think. But it didn't make sense in context. 'What recent proposals?' I asked myself. She (Snowling 1987) hadn't been writing about any recent proposals. So I re-read the sentence:

> The present proposals have fairly direct practical implications.

Ah-ha! Now I knew what she was writing about: the immediate things she'd just been dealing with. But how had I come to make this reading error? Four things are immediately obvious:

+ 'present' and 'recent' have letter sequences in common;
+ syntactically, both are adjectives;
+ semantically, both are to do with time in relation to the current moment;
+ 'The recent proposals... etc.' is a perfectly good English sentence; it was only its meaning in the context of the whole passage that was the problem.

It would make sense to guess that somewhere in the semantic system there is some overlap in the way the two words, 'recent' and 'present' are accessed, and that the overlap in their spellings exacerbated the situation, producing the error. Maybe we don't necessarily process all the letters in a word before identifying it. The acceptability of 'recent' in the sentence itself meant no problems emerged until, at some higher level of discourse comprehension, the whole thing didn't hang together. It was only at this highest level, which is the level of conscious attention to the coherence of the whole text, that anything occurred to suggest there was a problem requiring me to re-read the sentence.

As a matter of fact, my fingers on the book were half obscuring the word 'present', so that might explain why I didn't process all the letters, why I made a psycholinguistic guess that met some but not all of the required criteria. My attempt didn't quite work. But it could be that on other occasions I have misread words and never realised.

The situation is similar to that of the child who does not fully process the printed word and thus provides herself with degraded visual input – as with the girl who read 'shoe' for 'shop'. Compensating for incomplete visual processing may well give the wrong answer. And where monitoring for meaningfulness is also inadequate, the problems are compounded.

EXAMPLE 5

I suggested in relation to the last example that the substitution might be explained by degraded visual information. In the case of my next example, however, I had no such excuse. One could perhaps call it a motivated substitution.

As a student I was reading *Felix Holt* by George Eliot. Esther had met Felix in the woods and they were having a heated argument. As I recall, the passage went something like this:

> Although she was so angry she knew that she was being
> very pretty.

I liked this perception so much that I re-read the sentence:

> Although she was so angry she knew that she was being
> very petty.

Oh, I had misread 'petty'. I really should have known – George Eliot, the moralist, would, of course, say 'petty'. Maybe only the lighter, brighter and more sparkling Jane Austen might have been alert to the two levels of self-perception that 'pretty' seemed to suggest, and be willing to have a heroine who is both vain *and* self-aware.

It's clear enough, in one way, how my error had come about. After all, there's only one letter's difference. According to one theory of word identification all the possible candidate words that share the sequential letter features contained in the printed word are activated. The more visual information that is attended to, the more possible candidates are excluded. Clearly, in this case, all the shortish words beginning with 'p' that didn't also end with 'etty' had been eliminated. Only two candidates were left.

But I jumped the gun. Something in me thought that 'pretty' was the best candidate. Maybe it was sexism. Maybe I wanted Esther to be stereotypically feminine, concerned not about her own moral integrity ('petty') but about her appearance and possible effect upon Felix ('pretty'). Or maybe it wasn't sexism, it was just that I was simply reading for romance: I wanted Esther and Felix to fall in love. Whatever the motivation for this error, it seems two things were happening. The bottom-up processing of print was going on, putting up candidate words and at the same time top-down processing was seeking for plausible meanings. Somewhere between the two a spark jumped, giving the meaning I read first. In this case, however, the spark was a short circuit.

Of course, it could well be that the *real* reason I was impelled to re-read the sentence was not, as I thought, to savour some literary effect, but that, at some unconscious level, my bottom-up print processing caught up and registered the mismatch between the visual input and the word identified.

A CHILD'S EXAMPLE

So much then for these examples from my own reading experience. But do children work in the same kind of way? The answer seems to be, yes. Here is an example of an equally complex reading error by a child. This example is given by Bettelheim and Zelan (1991). A girl was reading aloud from *Black Beauty* and in the process read this passage:

> Then someone ran to our master's house and came back
> with a gun; presently there was a loud bang and a dreadful
> shriek, and then all was still; the black horse moved no
> more.

In the event, however, the girl misread 'dreadful'. She read it as, '...a loud bang and a deadful shriek...'

Bettelheim and Zelan report that when asked about what had happened in the story, the girl answered:

> 'The horse was shot because it had a broken leg.' 'Since the
> horse was shot,' we replied, 'its shriek certainly was
> deadful.' In reaction to this, she looked at the text and said,
> 'Oh, no, it says "dreadful".' (page 166)

Clearly the girl had understood that the horse had died and it seems that this semantic understanding had interfered with her reading aloud, thereby producing an unconscious error. She was not simply decoding the text, but her top-down processing had been going on at quite a sophisticated level, incidentally creating a semantically motivated error.

These examples, like all errors and self-corrections whether by adults or children, suggest the need for a theory to explain what is going on. And unless we understand what is going on, we are not likely to be able to help children with their reading as effectively as we might. What are some of the things that any such theory would need to explain? These are some of the issues our examples have raised:

✦ How do we identify words from print – letter by letter, or in whole words, or in chunks and letter sequences of various types?

✦ What is the role of phonological processes, for example, 'hearing' words pronounced in our heads, in word identification?

✦ What is the role of context in identifying words? There seem to be morphological, syntactic and semantic issues involved.

✦ At what level does comprehension enter into the system, and what is the place of phonological processing in comprehension? Why do we 'hear' what we read in the mind's ear?

✦ How do all the levels and processes work together? How do top-down and bottom-up processes work together seamlessly in fluent, accurate reading?

These, then, are some of the questions that a theory of reading will need to answer.

CONCLUSION

Reading is a skill that has become relatively effortless to most adults through overlearning. All the sub-skills that took so long and so much practice to learn become co-ordinated and automatised.

Yet the point of the examples in this chapter is to suggest how the largely unconscious processes of our sophisticated reading ability are themselves complex and interdependent. Even as adults we make errors which give us some insight into the processes. If we are to help children who are learning to read, we will be able to do so in a much more informed manner if we understand something of the processes that they are using and needing to develop. Their procedures, errors and self-corrections, to use Goodman's own metaphor (1973), give a window on to the processes they are employing. But to be able to make sense of the errors and self-corrections that we observe, we also need to have a clear model of the processes involved in reading.

Such a model will need to be able to describe the array of processes that the sophisticated adult reader possesses, together with the ways these processes interact to produce meaning from text. That is, it will need to provide a clear picture of the *goal* of reading development. Further, it will need to explain the processes of development that enable the pre-reading child, equipped with a spoken language system and a visual system, to bring these things together in a new system for making sense from print. It will need to be a *developmental* model, explaining the mechanisms of change and progress. Sketching out such a model is the subject of the next two chapters.

CHAPTER 3

MODELLING THE READING PROCESS

THE AIM OF THIS CHAPTER

In this chapter we will begin to construct an explanatory theoretical model of the reading process and, in particular, to present a framework for thinking about:

✦ the complementary contributions of top-down and bottom-up processing;

✦ the ways in which pre-reading language and visual discrimination skills come together and develop into reading processes;

✦ the crucial role phonological processing plays in both the developing and mature reading processes.

The theoretical model we are going to consider here is adapted from Marilyn Jager Adams (1990), who herself developed her model from the work of Seidenberg and McClelland (1989). The model provides a schematic picture of how different processes work together in reading. We will build up the full picture in a series of stages, each of which will be based on a flow diagram. The last diagram, incorporating the main elements from each stage, shows the whole model.

The aim of the model is to explain how we process printed words to make sense of them. This involves processes for identifying the words in the text and processes for selecting contextually relevant meanings. In reading the description of the processes, it is a good idea to refer back to the diagrams frequently and check that (hopefully!) they are growing in meaning and clarity. The model is intended to act as a general map that will orientate us and show us where we are throughout our discussion of the reading process in the rest of the book.

A SIMPLIFIED MODEL OF WORD IDENTIFICATION

Figure 1 represents a simplified view of our adult reading processes. It shows only one bottom-up and one top-down processor contributing to the production of meaning and represents the way individual words are identified and ascribed meaning. When we come to considering how we make sense of continuous text we will need to discuss things somewhat differently.

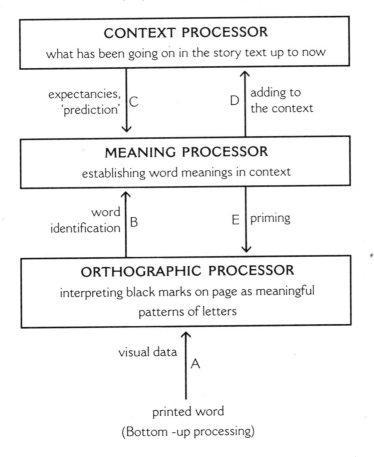

(Top-down processing)

CONTEXT PROCESSOR
what has been going on in the story text up to now

expectancies, 'prediction' C — D adding to the context

MEANING PROCESSOR
establishing word meanings in context

word identification B — E priming

ORTHOGRAPHIC PROCESSOR
interpreting black marks on page as meaningful patterns of letters

visual data A

printed word
(Bottom -up processing)

Figure 1

A simplified model of the reading process.

According to the constructivist ideas discussed in the previous chapter, we make sense of new knowledge in the light of existing knowledge. The Context Processor deals with existing knowledge: what, in general, we know about language and what we know about the world, and more particularly, what we know about the immediate textual context, how its grammatical structure is developing and what it seems to be about. The Orthographic Processor supplies new information: its task is to identify the words in the text from their spellings. The Meaning Processor makes sense of the new information by relating it to the existing knowledge about grammar, about word meanings and about the preceding text. The three processors are represented one above the other so that the Orthographic Processor may be seen as the bottom-up processing system and the Context Processor may be seen as the top-down processing system.

The arrows in the diagram represent the flow of information within the system. Thus, arrow A indicates that the Orthographic Processor receives information by way of the eyes from the print. The different processors themselves are in an interactive relationship, with information flowing both ways between them. The arrows going upwards represent bottom-up effects, and the arrows going downwards represent top-down effects.

THE ROLE OF THE MEANING PROCESSOR

The Meaning Processor receives information from the other two processors. When we are reading effectively we do not usually have to give much conscious attention to the other two processors but, in so far as we recognise a word-meaning, we are giving conscious attention to the Meaning Processor. There is a great deal, however, going on in the Meaning Processor below the threshold of consciousness. Its function is to identify a word-meaning unambiguously by co-ordinating information from the other two processors at an unconscious level and making that meaning available to our conscious attention. Thus, if we are reading the phrase *a row of buses*, we consciously think only of '*row* – things arranged in a line', and totally ignore any other meanings of the word *row* like 'a noisy argument' or 'propelling a small boat with the use of oars'.

THE ROLE OF THE ORTHOGRAPHIC PROCESSOR

The function of the Orthographic Processor is to process the visual information from the print on the page. The Orthographic Processor gets its name because it processes spellings. Its job is to receive the visual data from the printed page, and from this identify letters and recognise their sequential organisation. This information is processed into a suitable form to send up the line (arrow B) to the Meaning Processor to enable it to identify the word.

The Meaning Processor has access to the mental dictionary (or 'lexicon'). The entry in this mental dictionary for any particular word includes some kind of orthographic form or 'template' as well as the word's meaning. So for a known word the information from the Orthographic Processor is matched up with the existing 'template' in the dictionary and the word is identified.

THE ROLE OF THE CONTEXT PROCESSOR

As we saw with the phrase *a row of buses*, words are potentially ambiguous. Most of the commonest words in any language have a variety of different meanings and to identify a word is not necessarily the same thing as to identify its meaning in context. Some sort of selection from potential meanings has to be made in the light of the context.

When we read the word 'table' on its own, the meaning that is activated is probably its commonest meaning – 'a piece of furniture for putting things on and sitting round'. But, of course, the word can have other meanings: for example, it might refer to a tabulation of facts or numbers like the three-times table. If we are reading the word in the context of a book, information flows down (arrow C) from the Context Processor and an appropriate selection from the possible meanings of 'table' will be activated. For example, if we are reading a geography book, we may come across the phrase 'a table mountain' and, without thinking consciously about it, we select the meaning 'flat-topped with steep sides'. We will not think that the mountain has legs or is 'a tabulation of numbers'! Inappropriate responses are suppressed.

The Context Processor, then, may be said to help select appropriate responses from the field of possible responses activated by the orthographic form of the word. However, to talk about 'selecting' is misleading. There isn't a little person up there in the Context Processor who is selecting suitable meanings from the mental dictionary. Rather, we have to think in terms of mechanisms. The mechanism in this case is a neurological interaction between top-down and bottom-up effects, activating a particular meaning.

Let us consider our 'table mountain' example a little further. The word 'table' is identified and its whole set of potential meanings is activated. At the same time, the Context Processor has constructed an interpretation of what the passage is about; and this activates a set of potential meanings in the Meaning Processor. Where the two sets of potential meanings coincide, the effect is cumulative and is sufficient to thrust one meaning into consciousness.

INTERACTIVE PROCESSES

The explanation of the model (Figure 1) so far has dealt with the arrow up from the Orthographic Processor and the arrow down from the Context Processor. The Orthographic Processor identifies the word and the Context Processor determines its meaning in the context. But what about the arrows going in the reverse directions, both down and up from the Meaning Processor?

The arrow down from the Meaning Processor to the Orthographic Processor (arrow E) is the continuation of the context effects impinging on the Meaning Processor. It may be thought of as the influence of expectation upon the interpretation of what we see – and this would explain the kinds of errors we discussed in the previous chapter between 'petty' and 'pretty', 'present' and 'recent', and 'dreadful' and 'deadful'. A context can produce expectations that lead to an accelerated, hair-trigger response. This effect is called 'priming'.

Figure 2 overleaf represents the way a context can 'prime' word identification. The story context creates a wide field of expectancies. The word 'heard' limits the field to sounds and the word 'quiet' limits the field even further. These effects are semantic, or effects of word meaning. The grammar, or syntax, demands a noun. Meanwhile the Orthographic Processor is working on the print and identifying various letters and letter groups. These are matched up with word spellings in the mental dictionary. As it happens, all the letters have been processed effectively, so the word 'whimper' is identified. Since this meaning fits the context and makes sense, the criterion of coherence within the system has been satisfied. All the sources of information that we discussed in Chapter 1 – graphophonic, syntactic and semantic – are in accord.

However, it is worth noting that the word 'whisper' was also contextually primed, and was only one letter short of having its spelling fully identified. If the orthographic processing had been less efficient and the spellings of both 'whisper' and 'whimper' had been equally identified, the strength of the priming effect from the context might have determined which word was identified. Priming can lead to miscues – if, and only if, the orthographic processing of the spelling is not complete.

As for the arrow, in Figure 1, up from the Meaning Processor to the Context Processor (arrow D), what this represents is the contribution of newly identified meanings to the developing context of meaning in the Context Processor. This contribution will influence the Context Processor's field of activated meanings that in turn affects the *next* word meaning to be identified in the Meaning Processor. The context of meaning is continuously developing.

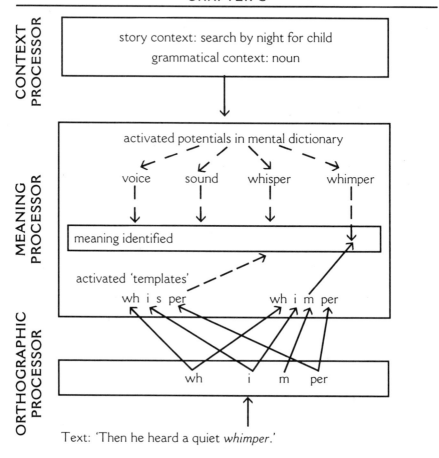

Figure 2

Contextual priming effects.

In considering Figure 1, we have used a simplified and incomplete model of word identification. It is simplified and incomplete in three ways. Firstly, the actual processes discussed here can be specified much more completely. Secondly, it is only concerned with word identification, not with comprehension of continuous text. Thirdly, there are elements in the reading process that this model simply does not touch on. The most vital of these is the role of phonological processing in reading. But the important concept this simplified model has highlighted is the complementary and interactive contributions of top-down and bottom-up processes in the making of meaning.

To some extent you could say that there is a race taking place between the top-down and bottom-up processes to see which can identify the word first! As it happens, in normal circumstances with experienced readers, the bottom-up route of orthographic processing tends to win by milliseconds. But with children who are learning to read, things can be different and the top-down effects can prompt 'prediction'. What is important for the learning process, however, is that the system is interactive. This provides compensating mechanisms for any shortfall in the information supplied by either the top-down or bottom-up processes and also provides a monitoring mechanism for errors if the sources of information aren't in accord. These monitoring processes can have a tutorial or self-teaching effect by drawing attention to errors.

PHONOLOGICAL PROCESSES

The simplified model that we have been discussing does not touch on the place of phonological processing in mature reading. Our experience, as we hear what we read in the mind's ear, shows that phonological processing is involved in the visual process of reading. When earlier in the chapter we discussed the words *row*, *row* and *row*, I imagine it probably troubled you slightly that I said that *row* (the line) and *row* (the angry dispute) were the same word with different meanings. Even though you were reading silently, their different pronunciations were part of your perception of the words.

As we have said, the mental dictionary records the meaning (meanings) of a particular word and also its orthographic form or template. Similarly, if a word is in our speech vocabulary, the dictionary must contain some kind of phonological representation or a sound-image of the word. The question arises, how and why, when we read silently to ourselves, do we seem to hear the words in our heads? Maybe when a word is read, the whole dictionary entry is activated, and the sound-image simply jangles to no special effect. But this seems unlikely. We seem to hear the words' spoken fluently, with expression in a meaningful intonation pattern. This intonation pattern, whether it assists in processing for meaning or is a result of it, suggests that the phonological image is no mere by-product of word identification. It is closely linked with making sense of what we read. This is an issue we shall return to.

At this moment, I want to consider the place of phonological processing in the total language system and how it helps to bring the orthographic processing system into existence. Let us start by looking at another model (Figure 3).

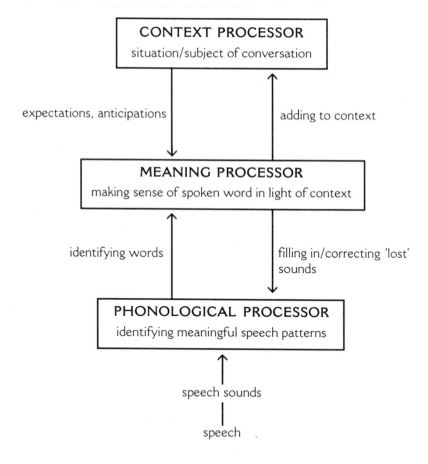

Figure 3

Model of spoken language system.

UNDERSTANDING SPOKEN LANGUAGE: THE PHONOLOGICAL PROCESSOR

Phonology is the study of how sound is systematically related to meaning in language. The Phonological Processor, then, is the name we give to the function of the auditory system that identifies and processes sounds and sound patterns that are linguistically meaningful.

Figure 3 represents the system by which we process spoken language. It works very much like the model represented in Figure 1, except that it deals with hearing, not seeing, and with phonological information and entries in the mental dictionary. But there is one big difference between the two models. While Figure 1 represents only a partial view of what is going on in a reader's mind because it has no phonological component, Figure 3 represents the *total* language system of a non-reader. Pre-reading children bring this whole operational language system with them to the task of learning to read.

For the pre-reader, then, language is the spoken language system. Learning to read is the creation of a new language system in the child, and this can only be achieved if the leading role is played by the existing phonological language system. As we have said, we only make sense of new information in the light provided by existing knowledge, and learning is the extension of the knowledge or mental structures and representations we already possess. For the beginning reader, when she encounters a written word, the only way in which she can assign it a meaning is if she is told what it means. It is not for nothing that we say of a written word or letter, 'it *says* so-and-so'. If printed language is ever going to mean anything to us, we have to learn it, in the first instance, through the phonological processes of spoken language.

LEARNING TO IDENTIFY NEW WORDS

When the child encounters environmental print and asks what it says, she is told that it says 'Kellogg's' or 'Asda' or whatever. At this early stage the child has not learned the letters nor that words have to be read left-to-right. The word is a complex pattern of marks and what the child picks on by which to identify it in future is to some extent arbitrary. Certain salient features may stand out. For example, one little boy learned to recognise the word *television* 'because it's got two dots'. Another little boy recognised the word *yellow* 'because it's got two sticks'. (Unfortunately he also identified the word *smaller* as 'yellow' because it had the same two sticks in the middle!)

At this first stage of whole-word 'reading' what the children are doing is learning the name of a visual pattern that they identify from certain arbitrary features. The visual processing the child is doing cannot yet properly be called orthographic processing, though the child is beginning to discriminate certain letter features.

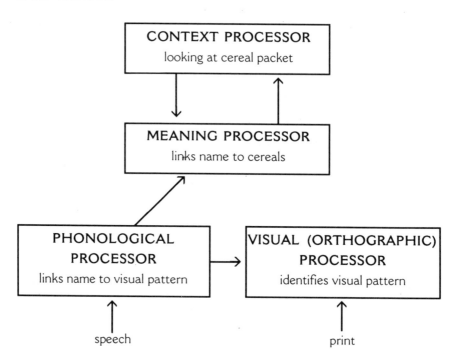

Figure 4

Learning new 'whole words' (I).

Figure 4 represents the steps by which a new sight-vocabulary word acquires meaning. There are no links upwards in it from the visual system to the Meaning Processor because the written word as yet means nothing to the child. When the child enquires, for example, what it says on the cereal packet, she is attending to the visual pattern of the print and there is an input to the Visual Processor. At the same time she hears the name 'Kellogg's'. This simultaneity establishes an association between the visual pattern and the sound-image of the word.

At this point in learning, then, the phonological system is giving linguistic significance to previously meaningless visual patterns. The patterns cannot yet be seen as spellings because the child doesn't know about letters and serial order. The printed words will be scanned like any other object, with the eye jumping back and forth between the details it picks on, building up a patterned image. The written word has no more logic to it for the child than a word in Arabic script is likely to have for most of us. As the Arabic word is to us, so the pattern of the written word is likely to be to the child: confusing and hard to remember. But the child doesn't have to remember it as a total pattern; the probability is that the child only remembers certain details and maybe the general size and shape. It is enough if she is able to pick out the same word another time using this limited information.

RECOGNISING NEWLY LEARNED WORDS

When the child encounters the word pattern again (or even misidentifies some other word as that pattern, as with *yellow* and *smaller*), the Visual Processor identifies the word and triggers the Phonological Processor. For example, Jack, aged three, looks at the new ketchup bottle and suddenly points and says in surprise, 'Asda!' He has only ever seen Heinz ketchup before, but evidently had learned the Asda logo from other things. Now he retrieves the name.

Figure 5 overleaf represents the situation of the child identifying the newly-learned word. There is now no speech input to the Phonological Processor, yet a phonological response is activated. Very quickly a link begins to build up directly between the Visual Processor and the Meaning Processor. And perhaps we can start to talk of the visual processing as 'orthographic processing' now that a print-word/pronunciation/meaning link has become established. We may feel more certain about talking of orthographic processing proper, however, when the child has learned the letters of the alphabet and directionality and then applies this knowledge in helping to identify words.

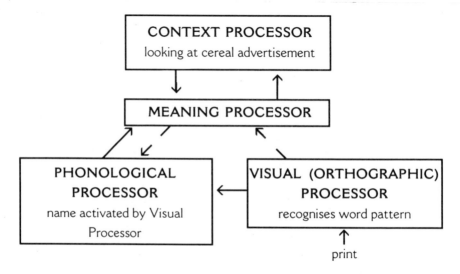

Figure 5

Learning new 'whole words' (2).

THE COMPLETE PROCESSOR MODEL

We have looked at certain aspects of the processor model so far, separating issues out in order to try to make them clearer. But now it is time to try to see the thing as a whole.

The complete model of the developed system is represented in Figure 6. Arrows now run both ways between the Phonological Processor and the Orthographic Processor, and both ways between each of them and the Meaning Processor. Because we are dealing with reading alone, there is no auditory input to the Phonological Processor. Any activation of the phonological processes will be in response either to the Orthographic Processor or to the Meaning Processor.

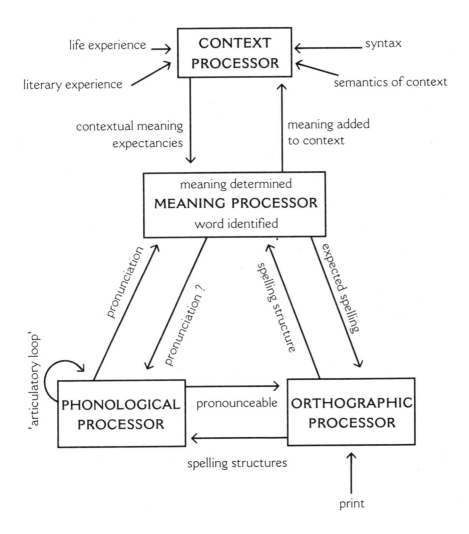

Figure 6

The complete model.

There are two possible routes by which meaning can be accessed from print – the direct route from the Orthographic Processor to the Meaning Processor, and the indirect route, going round by way of the Phonological Processor. A printed word can now, in principle, activate its meaning without recourse to phonological processes. So, for the skilled reader, a pseudo-sentence like 'Tell me wear he went', is nonsense. The meaning of 'wear' is accessed through its spelling orthographically. If the meaning were accessed phonologically through the phonological translation of the sentence, the sentence would make perfect sense. It would be indistinguishable from 'Tell me where he went'.

In fact, most children at about six years old *will* say that the 'wear' sentence makes sense, whereas most children at about ten years old will say it is nonsense (Harris and Coltheart 1986). It seems that the younger children access meaning by way of phonological translation, whereas the older children have more fully developed the orthographic route for accessing meaning. However, even as adults we still have the indirect route of phonological translation available to us – otherwise we wouldn't be able to understand why young children have problems with 'wear' and 'where'!

If the adult experience of hearing what we read in the mind's ear isn't simply a functionless 'appendix' left over from an earlier stage in the evolution in the reading system, what might its function be?

There are two main functions to consider. One is supporting the orthographic route in word identification. In this situation the Phonological Processor is activated by the Orthographic Processor. The Phonological Processor can determine whether a given written 'word' is pronounceable, and can check whether it is known as a spoken word.

The second function is to extend the short-term memory to facilitate comprehension when reading continuous text. It helps us to retain the words of a sentence until it can be interpreted. This is the significance of the small arrow in Figure 6 that loops out from the Phonological Processor and back into it again. It is called 'the articulatory loop'. There is no equivalent arrow on the orthographic side and it represents one of the most important functions of the Phonological Processor in the reading system. The short-term auditory memory for language is much more secure and longer lived than the visual orthographic memory for print. It is easier to hold a whole phrase, clause or sentence in memory in its internalised phonological translation than it is to hold a graphic memory of it. Since we cannot fully process the words of a sentence for meaning until it is complete, we need to be able to hold the words in store until this processing for meaning can be successfully undertaken.

THE MODEL IN PRACTICE

So much for the structure of the model. How does it actually work? The visual input from the print is processed in the Orthographic Processor, which sends information both to the Meaning Processor and to the Phonological Processor. In the Phonological Processor this information activates the relevant sound-images, and this new information is transmitted to the Meaning Processor. So, the Meaning Processor is stimulated by the Orthographic Processor both directly and indirectly by way of the Phonological Processor. The indirect route provides support to the direct route. Overall, it provides a fail-safe redundancy within the system, so that there is more than one way to identify the words that are encountered. These are some aspects of this redundancy:

◆ When the two routes are working in concert, the activation of the Meaning Processor is expedited – or at least, not hindered. There is scope for cross-checking and self-correction.

◆ While frequently encountered words (like *the* and *was*) have a strong direct orthographic link to the Meaning Processor, new and infrequently encountered words will not. Access by way of phonological translation may therefore assist in the identification of a word, either in the case of infrequently encountered words, by reinforcing the orthographic identification, or in the case of words encountered in print for the first time, by identifying it as a known sound-word.

✦ If a word (for example, *zoril*) is unknown even in its phonological representation, at least the unknown word begins to build up a phonological as well as an orthographic identity around which contextual and definitional meanings can start to coalesce. (By the way, a zoril is carnivorous – you can now start to build up a meaning for the word!)

✦ As we have seen with *homophones* like 'wear' and 'where', the orthographic system can help distinguish between phonologically ambiguous words. Conversely, the phonological system can sometimes help us distinguish between *homographs* like 'row' and 'row'. There is no orthographic clue as to what meaning is appropriate, but the Meaning Processor may be helped by the phonological system providing two different pronunciations that distinguish different meanings. Only the context, of course, will finally determine the appropriate choice.

Meanwhile, of course, all the top-down influences are working on the Meaning Processor. In this model we have specified a range of contextual effects within the province of the Contextual Processor. These may be divided into two general categories: those closely related to the immediate text, like syntax, and semantics relating to both the individual word and the immediate text; and those related to prior knowledge about life and literature. All of the effects may influence the speed of word identification and the particular meanings activated. They may also affect the comprehension of continuous text. Chapters 7 and 8 will deal with these issues in detail. For now it is enough to remark that syntax, together with semantic context, can help us to make sense of unfamiliar (Yorkshire dialect) words and usages, as in 'The rain were fair siling down.'

Similarly, general knowledge about the world and about what different texts are likely to mean will feed into children's reading expectancies. Thus the picture of a volcano may well prime the child to be able to read 'eruption' fluently, although she has never seen the word before.

These different kinds of contextual effects may do one of two things. They may help the child to identify words by joining forces with bottom-up processes or they may be used as an alternative to bottom-up processing and prompt linguistic guessing. As we have already indicated, linguistic guessing tends to characterise beginning and backward readers and, in adults, is generally a measurably slower process than processing the print. On the other hand, the mutual reinforcement of top-down and bottom-up processes strengthens the whole reading performance of a child. Orthographic processing is confirmed by the construction of coherent meanings and comprehension, and the meanings and comprehension that are established are built upon the solid rock of the actual wording of the text.

MUTUAL MODIFICATION BETWEEN PROCESSORS

We have already argued that the Phonological Processor is responsible for the development of the Orthographic Processor. There are also ways in which the Orthographic Processor develops phonological processes. For some children, seeing the separateness of words on the page helps them perceive the individual words in the streamy flow of speech, where the sounds of one word are often continuous with the next. But perhaps the most immediately relevant aspect of the orthographic contribution to phonological processes is the way in which learning the letters and spellings prompts new skills of phonological analysis. Phonemic awareness follows the learning of alphabetic skills rather than leading them. The visual identity of letters tends to alert children to the separate identity of individual phonemes. This is a theme that will recur in the next two chapters. In the reverse direction, phonological processes help in organising the perception of letter sequences within words, and thereby facilitate orthographic processes. This will be a major theme in Chapter 6.

CONCLUSION

In looking at the processor model we have seen the complementary contributions of top-down and bottom-up processing to the identification of words and their relevant meanings. We have seen something of the way that the child's visual processing skills and her spoken language system come together to create the new language system of reading. And we have commented on the way that phonological processing is not only instrumental in building up the reading system, but remains functional in that system, not least in facilitating the processing and comprehension of continuous text. But, since the model represents the process of word identification at one moment, it is not easy to use it to present the dynamics of change and development over a period of time. This will be the subject of the next chapter.

CHAPTER 4

DEVELOPMENTAL STAGES IN LEARNING TO READ

THE AIM OF THIS CHAPTER

A developmental model aims to give structure to what it seeks to explain, and so provide a picture that is not cluttered by, but absorbs the detail. It aims to get below the surface and highlight qualitative changes and the dynamics that drive development. But, as Linnea Ehri (1991) remarks, reading involves 'a host of processes operating together in concert' (page 63). A new process doesn't instantly take over, replacing earlier processes, but may be added little by little to the child's repertoire of reading strategies until it comes to take on the leading or dominant role. Consequently, the stages of development may not be very clearly demarcated, giving a 'messy' overall picture.

In this chapter we will first look at a common-sense descriptive model of reading development, and then follow this up with a more structured model that seeks to explain the deeper processes taking place.

A DESCRIPTIVE MODEL

The structure of this descriptive model is largely derived from Jeanne Chall, as adapted by Ehri (1991). This model posits four stages of reading development, starting with Stage 0 ('0' because it is a pre-reading stage).

STAGE 0: PRE-READING OR EMERGENT READING

This stage deals with what children already know before they receive any reading instruction. The children will have fairly well developed spoken language and, having been brought up in a literate society, many will have picked up a good deal of information about print and reading. From reading sessions with adults they will know and imitate many of the procedures of reading: holding the book, turning the pages, pointing to pictures and print, putting on a 'reading' voice and re-telling the story in bookish language. Listening to stories has developed their sense of story and their vocabularies. They will know some poems and nursery rhymes by heart and will probably be able to identify them in nursery rhyme books that are familiar to them. They will be alert to rhymes and alliteration and enjoy them.

They will probably also have learned to recognise various words they are familiar with in their environment: brand names and logos like 'Pepsi' and 'McDonald's'; shop names such as 'Harrods' or 'Asda' (depending on their environment!); road signs such as 'STOP' and 'NO PARKING'; labels in the classroom and very probably their own names. As time goes on they learn more and more 'sight vocabulary' words, including words they learn to recognise in favourite books.

If children can do all these things, although they cannot yet read, they are clearly interested and attuned in many ways to the process of reading. Such children are said to be *emergent readers* and they are ripe for instruction. At this stage, phonological awareness (for example, alertness to the sounds within words such as rhymes and alliteration) is a good predictor of later reading success.

Once in school, 'look-and-say' procedures and more structured book experience builds on their capacity to recognise whole words. In general, early reading of continuous texts is built on such 'sight vocabulary'. Marsh (1981) notes that this stage is characterised by 'rote learning' and 'linguistic guessing'. Such guessing is an extension of the 'play' or pretend reading they have indulged in earlier. At this stage, it is not always clear how far a child 'reading' a familiar book is guessing, inventing, remembering or recognising the words.

Of course, there are children who come to school with little preparation and background in literacy. Adams (1990) calculated that, in the United States, there might be a ten to twentyfold difference in relevant literacy experience between advantaged and disadvantaged children on entering school at six years old. Some children enter school ripe for reading, while others still have a long way to go. There is no reason to suppose that similar differences aren't to be found in the United Kingdom.

Before we move on to the next stage, it is worth noting that in this model no major distinction is made between 'pre-reading' and 'sight-vocabulary' skills. Perhaps it is not surprising that this model tends to discount sight-vocabulary skills as it derives originally from Chall, who is committed to phonics! In our second, more developmental model, sight-vocabulary reading is given much more significance as a stage in its own right.

STAGE 1: THE INITIAL READING OR DECODING STAGE

In the initial reading or decoding stage children learn how spellings represent the sounds and words of the spoken language. Under traditional phonics teaching, for example, they learn to sound out the letters, blend the sounds and so pronounce the words. Through instruction they begin to understand that letters represent phonemes, the smallest significant sound units in the language.

This enables them to identify words that are not already a part of their sight vocabulary. And, because they have now begun to grasp letter–sound correspondences and have learned left-to-right sequencing, they perceive their sight vocabulary words in new ways, relating spelling patterns with the sounds they know. The words they already know can act as models for tackling new words by analogy – identical spelling patterns within different words should sound the same. In this kind of way, phonological processing provides the child with a self-teaching mechanism.

Many of the frequently encountered words in the early

reading vocabulary are irregular, for example, *the*, *of*, *you*, *was*, *said*. One study suggests that of the 150 most frequently encountered words, only 35 are regular. Irregular words, by definition, don't lend themselves to simple phonics. Both for speed and accuracy, then, children still need to develop their sight vocabularies during this phase. So children at this stage have both sight vocabulary and phonological translation (recoding) strategies in their repertoire.

A further strategy that children employ, with increasing success, is to guess at words from context. The better readers tend to study words they find difficult, employing recoding strategies, while younger and more backward readers tend to prefer guessing at difficult words. A common strategy, and one that is much encouraged by teachers, is to sound the first letter phonologically, and then guess.

STAGE 2: THE FLUENCY STAGE

Normally children move into this stage during their second year of reading instruction. Fluency isn't just a matter of speed, though speed is very important. Among other things, fluency involves reading with appropriate expression. This depends upon comprehension as well as accuracy. To read a sentence with expression requires the child to have grasped the syntax and to know where the pauses and stresses should come within the sentence to highlight the meaning. Staccato word-by-word reading isn't fluent, however accurate it may be.

Reasonable speed in dealing with familiar and unfamiliar words is necessary for comprehension. This is because all the words of a sentence have to be present in the short-term memory at the same time for us to be able to process the sentence for meaning. While the struggling reader is stuck on a word, the earlier parts of the sentence are dropping out of the short-term memory. She loses track of where she was in the sentence and in the passage. This is why teachers encourage children to go back and re-read the sentence in order to incorporate the problem word within the flow of meaning.

Attaining fluency depends on the child working with texts that are at the right level to permit reasonable speed and yet are challenging. Marie Clay (1991) suggests that texts a child can read with 90–95 per cent accuracy are optimal. She also recommends that children be asked to re-read books they know well in order to reinforce their speed of processing and hence the development of their global comprehension of the text.

The challenges that a text may make are not necessarily related to word familiarity and decoding. Since fluency is in part dependent on grasp of syntax, it is important that the patterns of syntax in the texts are familiar to the child and not so complex as to overstretch the child's short-term memory. Since fluency in part also depends on comprehension, the meanings must be readily accessible to the child. The contents of early stories should be relatively familiar and predictable.

When all these textual criteria are satisfied, Frank Smith's (1978, 1985) dictum that 'children learn to read by reading' begins to make sense. Fluency develops with practice on material that is within the child's competence and from this practice, children develop the ability to read familiar words as rapidly as they can name single letters or digits. The end product of all this practice and self-teaching is such speed and effortless automaticity that the child's conscious attention is available for making sense of the text and thinking about it.

STAGE 3: READING TO LEARN

Hitherto, the child's task has been learning to read but, with greater fluency and automaticity in decoding, processing capacity is freed for more global comprehension of meaning. The child now has the ability to use reading, in Chall's phrase, to 'learn the new'. Thus, in the upper primary years, children are able to explore new and strange possibilities of experience by identifying with different characters in unfamiliar situations, as in fantasy, historical novels and tales of far-away places. They also discover the pleasures and uses of non-fiction and reference materials and, in the classroom, they can read increasingly complex instructions for themselves. Reading is no longer a task but a tool.

While, at the earlier stages of reading, measured intelligence was not the factor most closely associated with reading success, at this stage it is more highly correlated. This suggests that while the bottom-up processes, for example, those associated with phonological processing, are the most critical in the early stages of reading, at this later stage when certain basic reading strategies and techniques have been established, top-down processing for comprehension becomes more significant. This does not mean that the child is guessing at the text, compensating for poor bottom-up processing skills, but that she is better able to link the new with what she already knows, and thus develop her understanding.

The better equipped the child is in terms of word knowledge and world knowledge, and the better her reasoning skills, the better she will be in comprehending and remembering. The better at reading, comprehending and remembering the child is, the more she will read and the more her vocabulary and world knowledge will increase. For this reason, the gap between the attainments of the better and the worse readers progressively increases.

FRITH'S (1985) DEVELOPMENTAL MODEL OF READING

What we have been looking at so far has been essentially a descriptive model. It is now time to discuss a more structured model that goes into the underlying processes of reading development. The basic model that I am using (Figure 1) is an adaptation of Frith's (1985) model, influenced by Snowling's (1987) version. The first thing to notice is that reading and spelling are both represented in this model. This is because they are causally connected. Alphabetic (phonic) spelling precedes and has a facilitating effect upon the development of alphabetic reading; and orthographic reading precedes and facilitates the development of orthographic spelling. As Frith remarks,

age	reading	spelling
3?		
	logographic phase	(scribble-writing)
5?		alphabetic spelling
6?	alphabetic reading	
	orthographic reading	
10?		
		orthographic spelling

Figure 1

'Normal reading and writing development proceed out of step' (page 310).

Out of step, yes. But only because one leads the other.

Frith develops her model in terms of underlying strategies that children adopt. She argues that the stages in her model represent distinctive steps in development. We can observe discontinuities, and even apparent regressions, in individual children's reading progress. This suggests distinct changes have taken place deep within the processing system. She concludes:

> We can therefore assume that for reading there is a developmental sequence of steps, with new strategies introduced at different points in the sequence.

(pages 302–3)

THE LOGOGRAPHIC PHASE

The logographic phase is the initial stage of reading when children identify familiar words by sight from certain salient details. For example, 'McDonald's' may be recognised because of its distinctive 'M'. Letter order and phonological factors play no part in the process. The child names the word after recognising it, rather than recognising it as a result of pronouncing and so has no satisfactory strategy for tackling new words. If she attempts a new word at all, it will be either to misidentify it as some visually similar word she does know or to guess at it from the context.

Logographic skills seem to constitute the dominant strategy children employ during their first year of reading instruction. For this reason alone it seems sensible to count logographic strategies as 'proper' reading. 'Look-and-say' teaching procedures deliberately latch on to children's logographic capabilities. Whether they have been taught 'look-and-say' or not, children will have learned some words from environmental print and they will have been encouraged to identify whole words within the classroom when looking at books, labels and so on. Depending on how many words a child knows logographically, she may get quite a long way with early reading scheme books.

Logographic word identification is the start of the visual discrimination process that permits the later development of alphabetic and orthographic strategies. As Frith says, 'Each new strategy is assumed to "capitalise" on the earlier ones' (page 307). The value of logographic skills is not only that they enable children to derive sense from print, but that they also act as the foundation for future development when merged with other skills.

At this stage, children tend to have a very clear idea of what words they know how to read – and they don't feel responsible for reading words they don't recognise. It is as if they have a set of known-word pigeon-holes into which they try to fit any word they encounter, and fragmentary cues are enough to permit a pigeon-holing. Thus, in the example we looked at in Chapter 3, *smaller* was instantly assigned to the *yellow* pigeon-hole on account of its having 'two sticks' in the middle. Another child identified any word with a 'k' in it as saying 'black'. Children at this stage perceive the task as simply to discriminate sufficient visual information about a word to be able to categorise it into one of the existing pigeon-holes. If they can't fit it into any known-word pigeon-hole, they tend to ignore it. This pigeon-holing system is technically known as 'the discrimination net' (Marsh 1981; Harris and Coltheart 1986).

There is no intrinsic means in this process by which the child can add to her reading vocabulary. The only way a new word can be learned is as a result of being introduced to it – that is, as a result of some outside instruction, deliberate or accidental. When such instruction occurs, the child picks on the critical visual features by which she will recognise the word in future. Even when the teacher teaches new words with flash cards, she does not control what features of the word children will latch on to for purposes of discrimination. She can, however, try explicitly to draw attention to specific letter features.

If during her first year of reading instruction the child is learning the letters of the alphabet, it is likely that she will progressively come to use letters and combinations of letters within words by which to identify them. Word shape and length tend to be of much less, and reducing, significance. Seymour and Elder (1985), demonstrating the relative insignificance of word shape or outline, showed that different arrays of the letters in the word 'yellow', for example, only marginally affected children's ability to read the word. Thus, with the normal configuration, 'yellow', 66.3 per cent of the children could identify the word correctly. When it was displayed in a zigzag configuration, breaking up its outline, as shown below, 60.4 per cent could identify it.

```
    y       l       o
        e       l       w
```

When it was presented vertically, 49.7 per cent were successful.

```
    y
    e
    l
    l
    o
    w
```

Both Marsh (1981) and Seymour and Elder (1985) argue strongly that the discrimination-net process of word identification is the dominant one in the first year of children's learning to read. And this process comes to be more and more a matter of discriminating letters in some sort of order.

Over time, then, the criteria for the discrimination net change, becoming fuller and more letter-oriented. It seems likely that both teacher instruction and learning to write progressively alert children to letters as units, to directionality (the scanning of print from left-to-right) and to regular sequences of letters. As the letters and letter sequences come to be associated with the constituent sounds in words, development moves into another stage.

THE ALPHABETIC PHASE: SPELLING

During their first year of reading instruction children tend to read using logographic strategies but, when it comes to writing, things are different. Writing has to be undertaken a letter at a time. While mechanical copy-writing can be undertaken without reference to the individual letter sounds along the way, little will be learned if no phonological processing is going on. The alphabetic phase depends upon learning not only the letters of the alphabet, but also the alphabetic principle that letters correspond to sounds. The child needs to learn both the shapes of the letters and the sounds that they represent. Learning the alphabet takes place alongside logographic reading, and learning the alphabet is enhanced by writing the letters as well as looking at them. Independent spelling is regulated by sounding out the letters to be written, and so the nature of the alphabetic principle is reinforced.

The alphabetic principle is that letters stand for sounds, and consequently that letter–sound correspondences provide a way (not always successful!) of coding sound-words into print and print-words into sound. However, the perceptual analysis of word-sounds into their component phonemes does not come spontaneously to children. Furthermore, because children already have the tolerably effective logographic strategy available to them for reading, they don't experience any striking need to supplant it with alphabetic processes. The development from logographic to alphabetic reading processes isn't spontaneous.

The situation with writing, however, is different. There is no existing process to replace. Writing is a slow, letter-by-letter business, and in writing letters one at a time in sequence the child's attention is drawn to the principle that letters represent the sounds *within* words. If children are to try to spell for themselves, or try to remember spellings, they have to do it by 'phonological conversion' or translation of sound into print. This requires analysing the sound of words into their constituent sound segments – the phonemes.

Phonological segmentation is, in fact, a more complex process than it was thought to be when Frith proposed her model, and it is an issue we will come back to. But, for the moment, the points to stress are these:

✦ Writing and spelling introduce children to the alphabetic principle because they don't work without it.

✦ Reading works well enough without it, employing logographic/discrimination-net strategies.

✦ Writing and spelling focus attention on letter order, letter sounds and letter shapes.

✦ In writing and spelling children will typically write words they already know how to read logographically, but now they have to process the words they know differently, sound by sound and letter by letter.

✦ This process goes on, whether or not the child is being taught phonics concurrently as a reading strategy.

During the second half of their first year of reading instruction, then, children are likely to be using logographic strategies for reading, but alphabetic strategies for spelling. One result of this mismatch between spelling and reading processes is that children tend to be able to read some words they cannot spell, and spell some words they cannot read (Goswami and

Bryant 1990). Nevertheless, the alphabetic writing strategies are reinforcing letter–sound correspondences and the development of phonemic segmentation skills. When the child reads back a word she is writing to find where she has got to and what comes next, she is training herself in alphabetic reading skills. The seeds of development are being formed.

THE ALPHABETIC PHASE: READING

The alphabetic phase depends, of course, on the child knowing the letters of the alphabet. This means, being secure about letter identities and knowing what sounds they represent. But *using* this knowledge doesn't necessarily follow directly upon *acquiring* this knowledge. After all, the child already has a working sight-vocabulary system for reading. At first, knowing the alphabet may simply add more nameable details to the discrimination net.

In reading, the alphabet phase proper is characterised by children using letter–sound relationships for tackling unfamiliar and new words. More specifically, Frith (1985) defines it in terms of grapheme–phoneme correspondences, where graphemes (for example, the letter *m*, or the digraph *ch*) represent their respective phonemes. Frith's account of alphabetic processing is effectively a description of traditional phonic reading strategies where the word has to be pronounced before it can be recognised. Such processes depend upon being taught – Frith says that here, at least, some explicit instruction would seem to be necessary. One reason for this is that phonemic discrimination doesn't seem to come naturally to children, but depends upon and follows instruction in the alphabet. Another reason is that the more complex 'context-sensitive' rules, like the soft *c* rule and the silent *e* rule, are counter-intuitive.

Frith, like Chall and others, is concerned with grapho-phonemic processes but, for the reasons discussed in Chapter 2, it is more useful to use Goodman's term 'graphophonics' because it embraces 'grapho-phonemics' but is wider in scope.

It leaves open the possibility that phonological conversion does not necessarily depend solely upon the one-bit-at-a-time processes of grapho-phoneme conversion. There are good reasons for believing that there are other graphophonic processes in addition to grapho-phonemic decoding to be taken into account. In particular, the work of Usha Goswami (1991, 1993, 1994; Goswami and Bryant 1990, 1992) suggests that the use of analogies between known and unknown words is a powerful process of spontaneous self-teaching among very young readers. Such processes can, however, easily be assimilated into an extended version of Frith's model, as the next chapter will show.

The terms 'graphophonics' and 'phonological recoding', then, cover a range of ways of mapping sounds on to spellings. If phonological strategies supersede logographic ones, it is not simply a matter of replacing them, but in some way colonising them and taking them over. There is, Frith says, a process of 'merging' the strategies. The new information derived from phonological mapping facilitates the visual processing of words, transcending the existing logographic discriminations. The discrimination net is transformed, becoming both more complete and more meaningful as visual features of the word come to represent the sounds of the word.

To summarise some of the key features of alphabetic processing: learning the letters facilitates the perception that spellings represent sounds; the phonological discipline of spelling trains orthographic processing in systematic directionality; and orthographic segmentation and directionality train phonological processing in phonemic discrimination. These processes develop:

✦ the ability to read new words by applying spelling–sound correspondence rules;

✦ the processing of words as letter sequences;

✦ the recognition of frequent letter sequences in letter-strings;

✦ the association of specific letter sequences with salient sound chunks;

✦ the processing of letter-strings in phonological chunks.

THE ORTHOGRAPHIC PHASE

The orthographic phase is the phase of skilled reading where words are identified from their spellings virtually instantaneously. Of course, children entering this stage during Key Stage 2 still have a long way to go in developing their reading vocabularies, but the orthographic processing strategies are largely in place.

This phase begins with reading and spelling out of step. It is now reading that leads the way, not spelling. Spelling continues for quite a while as primarily an alphabetic/phonological process but reading develops new processes.

Reading is typically accomplished by visual word identification based on either whole word recognition or the analysis of words into known spelling chunks, which are then put together to make the whole word. In either case, all the letters are registered in their relationships to each other within spelling patterns. In this way, the orthographic process is visual and instant, like logographic reading, but it is more discriminating and accurate because it processes all the letters in a word in their serial order. It has taken over this complete and orderly procedure from alphabetic processing, including the chunking according to spelling but it bypasses phonological recoding as the route for identifying the word. Identification is dependent upon spelling, as we saw in the difference in response between six- and ten-year-olds to the phonologically ambiguous sentence, 'Tell me wear he went'.

SUMMARY

Frith's model of reading development distinguishes three phases. In phase 1, the logographic phase, children learn to identify whole words from partial cues (the details they latch on to). This process is essentially rote-learning, and does not provide any word-attack strategies for coping with new words. Progressively, as children become familiar with the alphabet, the salient features they use to identify words they know tend more and more to become letter patterns. Phase 2, the alphabetic stage, is characterised by phonic and other strategies for translating print into sound in order to access meaning. Knowledge of the alphabet makes it possible to tackle new words independently, whether by phonics or by analogy. This leads to an alertness to repeated spelling patterns within words as they are related to pronunciations. In phase 3, the orthographic phase, the routines of the alphabetic stage (processing all the letters in sequence) facilitate the learning of spelling patterns and the identification of words directly from their spellings. At different stages writing, and then reading, take the leading, initiating role in development.

GOSWAMI AND BRYANT'S VIEW ON THE CAUSES OF DEVELOPMENT

Not everyone agrees that development progresses by steps and stages. Using Frith's model as a springboard, Usha Goswami and Peter Bryant (1990) argue that by and large reading development is a single process at which children get progressively better:

> We think that a great deal of the development takes the form of children just getting gradually better at strategies which they use right from the start. (page 147)

They want to expand the issues that Frith (1985) raised about the causes of change and development. Instead of three phases, they talk of three causes. The first causal factor is phonological. Before children begin reading, they are very much aware of the sounds of words and how they relate to each other, for example, by rhyme and alliteration. When they meet print, they notice that component spelling patterns tend to correspond with component sound patterns in words, and this leads to their making inferences about spelling and using analogies to help tackle new words.

The second causal factor is the experience of coming to grips with the alphabet. The experience of reading and writing, as we have suggested earlier, alerts children to the existence of phonemes. Goswami and Bryant place great emphasis on the role that writing and spelling play in leading children towards phonemic processes in reading. The application of phonemic awareness in the first instance, however, is only made to the task of writing.

The third causal factor picks up Frith's ideas about the relationship between reading and spelling. Goswami and Bryant are impressed by the way that reading and spelling seem to develop independently of each other during the first two years of a child's learning to read. When these two processes eventually link up, a qualitative change takes place – the nearest thing to a 'step' in their theory. The two processes mutually facilitate each other.

These causal factors extend the scope of the fundamental capacity to draw analogies and make inferences about the relationships between sounds and spelling patterns. As children become more and more experienced, they become better and better at making valid inferences and analogies.

Central to both Frith's model and Goswami and Bryant's suggestions are the roles of phonological and orthographic processing, and the relationship between them. It is to these two processes that we turn in the next two chapters.

CHAPTER 5

PHONOLOGICAL PROCESSES

THE AIM OF THIS CHAPTER

Some of the most interesting work in recent years with regard to understanding the development of reading relates to the place of phonological processes in the development of orthographic processing. In this chapter we will look in particular at learning by phonological analogy and at phonics.

To take phonological awareness first, research findings include:

> Normal two-and-a-half-year-olds can detect and produce rhymes easily – and with evident pleasure! (Chukovsky 1963)

> With English three-year-olds, rhyme detection predicts reading success more than three years later. It also predicts later phonemic awareness. Both rhyme detection and phonemic awareness predict reading success independently of each other. (Goswami and Bryant 1990)

> With English four- to five-year-old non-readers, alertness to rhyme and alliteration predicts reading ability and spelling ability three and more years later even when controlled for intelligence. (Bryant and Bradley 1985)

> Controlled groups trained over two years from six to eight showed auditory rhyme and alliteration training had a beneficial effect on reading. But where this training was combined with exploring the words visually at the same time the benefits were much greater. (Bryant and Bradley 1985)

What these findings suggest overall is that, as Goswami and Bryant (1992) say, 'Phonological awareness is a powerful causal determinant of the speed and efficiency of learning to read' (page 49). Further, while phonological awareness occurs spontaneously in children, it is susceptible to development through experience and training.

Bryant and Bradley (1985) distinguish between two phonological awareness skills, both relevant to decoding:

> One is to work out the sounds in words. The other is to put
> words into categories... which share a common sound.
> (page 67)

That is to say, one skill is phonemic segmentation, the other is alertness to rhyme, alliteration and so on. As we touched on earlier, phonemic awareness (the ability to analyse word sounds into their smallest sound units) seems to be the result of the interaction between instruction in alphabetic skills and phonological sensitivity. Cross-cultural studies by Morais (1991) and others show that, without explicit alphabetical instruction, people are not analytically alert to the component phonemes in words – although, of course, they have been responding to phonemically marked distinctions of meaning all their speaking lives. Unreflective responsiveness to phonemic distinctions and analytic reflectiveness about sound-strings are very different skills with very different implications, especially in relation to phonics. Peter Bryant (1993), reviewing the experimental evidence, says that as far as phonemic awareness is concerned, 'children have to surmount a phonological barrier' and that the evidence suggests that 'it is entirely up to teachers to remove the barrier to explicit awareness of phonemes' (page 87).

The other aspect of phonological awareness, alertness to rhymes and so on, develops spontaneously, and is enhanced by auditory experiences like the rhythm, alliteration and rhyme in nursery rhymes that draw deliberate attention to the *sounds*, as distinct from the *meanings*, of words. Since alertness to rhymes is spontaneous in normal children and precedes learning to read, we will tackle this aspect of phonological awareness first.

ONSET AND RIME

Rhyme and, to a lesser extent, alliteration are surprisingly important elements in phonological processes. They relate very closely to the two smallest sound segments that children seem to be alert to spontaneously. The sound segments are called *onset* and *rime*, and these linguistic terms are used to distinguish the two parts of a syllable (a syllable consisting of a vowel sound with whatever consonant sounds go with it). Any consonant sounds that come before the vowel constitute the onset. The vowel sound and any consonant sounds that follow it constitute the rime. The table below illustrates this distinction between onsets and rimes.

onset	rime
–	am
l	amb
pr	am
st	amps

It is important to remember that the concepts of onset and rime refer to *sounds* in the first place, and not to spellings – though, of course, we have to represent the sounds with spellings when writing about them! These two parts of a syllable, onset and rime, are collectively called *intrasyllabic units*, because they are units *within* a syllable.

As is clear from their sensitivity to alliteration and rhyme, children are able to *identify* onsets and rimes, but they do not spontaneously *analyse* them any further. Onsets and rimes are the fundamental units of speech-sounds perceived by the alphabetically untutored child.

Clearly, it is rimes that rhyme. With onset and alliteration things are not so clear-cut. The onsets of 'sing', 'sting' and 'string' are different, yet we would say that they alliterate. Nevertheless, it does seem that alliteration, which is so basic to poetry, may also be basic to phonological processing in certain ways. Alliteration is characterised by emphasis on the initial phoneme. Phonic spelling requires the untangling of consonant blends, but where the child is not yet capable of this, the initial consonant sound of the blend tends to be dominant. This shows itself typically in young children's invented spellings where consonant blends are represented by a single consonant, for example, 'pam' for *pram*.

Onset and rime are important because they give children spontaneous and self-generated access to spelling–sound relationships. Since they are speakers before they are readers, their initial grip on words is phonological and it is in terms of their sound-images that children initially access meaning. Since children are alert to onset and rime, and are alert to salient features in the graphic form of words they know, it should not be surprising if they become alert to the regularities in print that correspond with the sound units they perceive. As Bryant and Bradley (1985) remark:

> It is probably a very short intellectual step from knowing that 'light', 'fight', 'sight' and 'tight' all end in the same sound, to understanding that that is why they all share a common spelling pattern. (page 67)

One of the earliest ways in which children develop phonological strategies to help in word identification is to identify the initial letter sound. One reason might be that, once directionality is learned, the initial letter is the first letter one comes to, so it is salient. But also, since sound is involved, it seems likely that onset-awareness is involved in initial letter–sound processes. This strategy works well, and is encouraged by teachers, because the initial letter in a word is usually a consonant. Typically, consonants are more reliable than vowels in terms of their sound-values, which makes phonic translation unproblematic. For example, consider the following words: *bat*, *bath*, *bathe*. Depending on your accent, there are either two or three different phonemes represented by the vowel *a*. The digraph *th* represents two different phonemes. But *b* remains a reliable constant as far as pronunciation is concerned.

Further, an initial single consonant, being an onset, is easy to segment, and this, together with the child's experience of the regularities of alliteration, facilitates the learning of the letter–

sound correspondence. Thus, onset status facilitates grapheme–phoneme correspondence learning. While grapho-phonemic skills depend primarily upon instruction, onset awareness and consequent spontaneous learning by analogy is a self-teaching mechanism. The identity of the initial consonant with the onset of the word is a potent support for graphophonic learning.

But more important still, we need to consider how the initial sound acts as a cue to guessing the word. The pronunciations of words in the mental dictionary are stored in terms of the phonological analyses children make. They must therefore initially be stored in terms of onsets and rimes. It is, then, the letter sound *as onset* that is the cue to guessing the rest of the word.

This will be true of single-phoneme onsets. But, as Treiman and Zukowski (1991) have shown, while children of five, six and seven years old distinguish both onset and rime, they find rimes easier to deal with than onsets *with blends*. It is in relation to rime that the clearest and greatest amount of research has been done.

RIME AND READING: LEARNING BY ANALOGY

Rebecca Treiman (1992) argues that children are not only spontaneously alert to the intrasyllabic units of onset and rime but that they readily infer links between the sounds they hear and spelling patterns they see in words. This mapping of sound to spelling is greatly assisted by one of the characteristics of English spelling – with rimes, spellings relate fairly consistently with pronunciations. For example, *-ang* and *-all* are relatively reliable as to pronunciation, though *sa-* and *ca-* are not (cf. *sang, say, said; car, care, cat*). Children's natural propensity to recognise rhymes maps usefully on to one of the more consistent aspects of English spelling–sound correspondence.

It is the work of Usha Goswami, working with Peter Bryant, that has suggested the significance of rime in particular. Both Marsh and Frith had discussed the place of analogy in learning to read, but they had both considered it a late development, belonging to the orthographic phase. Goswami, however, has shown that children in the early alphabetic phase can spontaneously identify new words by analogy with known words, using rime as the linking principle. It is recognising commonality of *sounds* that sets the process going in the first place, not perceiving commonality of spelling – though, of course, both have to be perceived together before analogies can function. Goswami (1993) considers the possibility that:

> ...a child's phonological knowledge might actually affect that child's analysis of printed words. A child who was good at rhyming might realise that shared sounds often mean shared spelling patterns, and that words like 'cat' and 'hat' not only rhymed, they also shared an orthographic unit ('-at').
>
> (pages 313–4)

However, perceiving common spelling patterns does not necessarily mean analysing the spellings. It means recognising certain chunks of spelling as a pattern. Thus, as Frith (1985) observed, children find it easier to recognise *nght* than *nite* as saying 'night'. It seems as if the *ght* combination in a terminal position in a word is characteristic enough to be identified with the rime /ight/. We may have a situation with early, unalphabetically skilled readers, where we are dealing with rime recognition from partial cues. The child's certain grip on the rime-sounds gives her some sort of visual grip on the common graphic pattern that represents the sound. This grip begins to establish sub-word visual recognition units.

The key to the process of learning by analogy is the rhyming of rimes. Goswami employed a 'clue' word technique in her investigations. She showed children a clue-word, for example 'beak', and told them what it said. Then she showed them other words and asked them to read them. What she found was that children could readily now read words like 'weak' and 'peak', but the clue-word did not help at all with words like 'bark' and 'bank'. The significance of the selection of test words was that they all shared the same number of phonemes in common with the clue-word. It was the configuration of the phonemes that was different. Where they formed a rime unit and the words rhymed, self-teaching by analogy became possible, but where they were scattered throughout the word and there was no rhyme, no self-teaching ensued.

While not so striking in its outcome, similar effects were found with onsets. A similar clue-word technique was used. Consonant blends were deployed in two situations, as the onsets of words and as the final consonant sounds in a word (that is, not the whole rime). It was found that, for example, the clue-word 'trim' enabled children to read 'trap', and 'flan' enabled them to read 'flop'. But on the other hand, 'desk' did not enable them to read 'risk', and 'wink' did not enable them to read 'tank'. In both this case and the case of the rimes, the possibility of transfer of learning by analogy only occurred where the sounds involved constituted a whole intrasyllabic unit, either the whole of the onset or the whole of the rime.

This, of course, fits in well with the notion of the sound-image of words in the mental dictionary being stored initially in terms of onset and rime. The consonant blend as onset is a phonological recognition unit, but the same blend at the end of a word is less than a whole rime and so does not constitute a phonological recognition unit with regard to rimes in the mental dictionary. Similarly, children make more analogies between words like 'beak' and 'peak' than between words like 'beak' and 'bean'. New reading analogies take place in terms of known phonological units.

Before we accept this model as a means of self-teaching, we have to consider how it might apply in everyday reading. In Goswami's test situations, the clue-words remained visible, so comparisons of spellings were readily available. In ordinary practice, clue-words will not be available in the same kind of way. The child will presumably need to consult internalised visual models. These models will be a half-way house between the salient graphic features of logographic reading and the patterned spelling knowledge of the orthographic phase. Not only does the analogy model of learning explain processes of self-teaching in phonological recoding, but it also suggests an account of one way in which visual processing develops, under the influence of phonology, from logographic towards orthographic processes.

BEYOND ONSETS AND RIMES

Following on from the observation that a small analogical transfer of learning took place between words like 'beak' and 'bean', Goswami (1994) employed her 'clue-word' investigations in three experiments with children of reading ages 6.5 years, 6.10 years and 7.6 years old. With the first group the expected rime-analogy pattern emerged: beginning readers only transferred pronunciations corresponding to rimes in words (for example, bug → rug). With the second group it was found that, although to a lesser extent than with rime-analogy, pronunciations for vowel and onset-vowel units were also transferred (for example, beak → heap, beak → bean). Vowel only transfer was significantly the smaller effect. With the third group, these findings were confirmed, but it also became clear that vowel transfer was restricted to vowel digraphs: single vowel transfers did not take place.

These findings were interpreted as indicating that as children become better readers, more complex patterns of analogical transfer take place, indicative of emergent phonemic decoding. Spelling chunks representing rimes and onsets become established as phonological recognition units first but, with more experience, onset-vowel clusters also become established as recognition units. This implies greater phonemic underpinning as it requires segmentation of the rime. Transfer based on vowels only, while it did take place, did so only with vowel digraphs like -ea-, not single letters. It is as though the digraph were perceived more strongly as a unit than individual letters. This suggests that frequency of serial letter *associations* might be a factor – a suggestion that we shall discuss further in the next chapter.

Goswami's interactive model of learning to read that reading development can be characterised as a increasingly refined phonological-orthographic analogy is perceived as a seamless process of development beginning, through which children make progressivel, subtler inferences about the mapping of sounds on to spellings. As reading develops and is explicitly taught, the phonological underpinning that was initially based upon onsets and rimes increasingly comes to reflect phonemic knowledge. This is a process largely of analysing *down* to phonemes, not building *up* from phonemes as most other models of reading development suggest. The processes of inference by analogy arguably might refine recognition units within words until a complete phonemic underpinning is established.

LEARNING BY ANALOGY

While, in the past, analogy models of learning have either only been seen as applying to later stages of development (for example, by Marsh and Frith) or have received something of a drubbing (for example, Patterson and Morton 1985), Goswami and Bryant have returned the idea to respectability, and shown it has a place in the early stages of reading. Patterson and Morton complained, 'the procedures for creating appropriate segments needed to access appropriate analogy words remain as yet unspecified' (page 355). Goswami has shown that onset and rime are two such 'appropriate segments'. What is more, since these phonological segments pre-exist the beginnings of reading, reading theory does not need to explain their origins. They are simply already there, ready to be used. Goswami has further suggested how more finely grained recognition units than onset and rime may be derived by analogical inference. The segment that we do need to explain is the phoneme.

TRADITIONAL PHONICS APPROACHES

Marilyn Jager Adams (1990), reporting and updating the work of Chall in relation to traditional phonics, concludes that:

Systematic phonics result(s) in significantly better word recognition, better spelling, better vocabulary and better reading comprehension at least through the third grade. (page 38)

The best predictors of reading success in first grade, regardless of instructional approach, are the children's prior ability to name both the upper and lower case letters of the alphabet, followed by auditory phoneme discrimination and general intelligence. (page 43)

Approaches in which systematic code instruction is included alongside meaning emphasis, language instruction, and connected reading are found to result in superior reading achievement overall. (page 49)

The success of systematic phonics teaching recorded here should not be interpreted as meaning that this is the ideal method of teaching reading. What the findings do strongly suggest is that phonics touches on a vital element in learning to read that children are perhaps deprived of with some other approaches. The important thing about phonics may well be its deliberate focusing of attention on the codes of sound–spelling correspondence but, as we have seen, there is more than one way to map sounds on to spellings.

THE ALPHABET AND PHONEMIC SEGMENTATION SKILLS

Synthetic phonics, involving the blending of individual letter sounds in a word, pre-supposes alphabetic knowledge at a more complete level than learning by analogy does. While learning by analogy involves recognising spelling chunks, synthetic phonics requires the easy recognition of all the letters in the word individually. This recognition involves both visual and phonological processes since the letters represent the sounds of the language. While it seems obvious that, for purposes of phonological recoding, learning the sound values of letters should have priority, the evidence Adams (1990) cites seems to be for learning letter names first. This is because, for the child to grasp the relationship between letter and sound, she first needs a clear mental representation of each.

Establishing the visual identity of letters is facilitated by giving them names. The name provides a clear conceptual identity for the letter around which experiences, both visual and auditory, can coalesce. A child, learning the letters, may perceive a c as a 'broken "o"'. But, of course, she should not mentally 'mend' c into o when dealing with print – even if we sometimes have to do it with handwriting! Being told, and learning, the letter name c gives it its own distinctive identity, separate from o. Naming is itself a phonological skill, and the ability to recognise that G and g are the same letter depends on naming because they are not the same shape. The name, as distinct from the shape or the sound, is unchanging and a reliable 'handle' on the letter.

Clearly letters can be (and generally are!) taught in terms of their sound values rather than by name. If we do so, we have to distinguish between 'kicking k' and 'curly c' to avoid some sorts of ambiguities; but we are still left with others such as 'The first "cuh" says "suh" in circus'. However we do it, the crucial requirement for reading is easy familiarity with the letters, their instant identification. Naming them is helpful in this and seems to mediate the relationship between letter form and sound value. Children who are not secure in visual letter identification are at a permanent and cumulative disadvantage.

Learning to hear the sounds of the letters in words is a problem in its own right. Hearing initial sounds is relatively easy – otherwise alphabet books saying 'a is for apple' and so on would not work. But phonemes within words are a different matter. As we have seen, this kind of analysis is not spontaneous. It is experience of the visual segmentation of letters, especially in writing, that prompts fine-grained phonological segmentation. As children's invented spellings show (for example, *plat* for 'plant', *wot* for 'won't'), it takes time and active experience of writing and written language before children *hear* all the individual phonemes in words. Though they may learn letter-sounds by rote, children have to operate with them for some time before the letters become fully meaningful to them.

SYNTHETIC PHONICS

Marilyn Jager Adams (1990), in her major review of all aspects of phonics and early reading instruction for the US Department of Education, supports many aspects of phonics teaching – but not 'phonics first and fast'. She insists that the alphabetic system of spelling–sound correspondences should be taught explicitly and early, and that training in phonemic awareness should be one of the earliest items on the agenda for First Grade students. She values highly the contribution that early independent writing with invented spelling can make to reading skills and sees the relationship between spelling patterns and speech-sound patterns as a central issue. Yet she points out that phonics teaching is too slow, mechanical and meaningless to be a satisfactory system of instruction on its own. We could perhaps interpret her conclusions as saying, not 'phonics first and fast', but 'phonics second and supportive'.

There are many different approaches to phonics. We shall consider just one system, the linguistically sophisticated *Phonics 44*, developed by Joyce Morris, the leading English exponent of traditional phonics teaching. It gets its name from the 44 phonemes in 'received pronunciation', or 'BBC English'. This system informed her reading scheme *Language in Action* (1974).

For teaching purposes the letters are grouped together so as to highlight contrasting features and thus facilitate visual discrimination between them. But there is a mismatch between the letters (26 of them) and the 44 phonemes of English. There are, for example, only five vowels but 20 different vowel sounds. Without considering the problems created by regional accents, Morris identified, in looking at her sample of the 3,000 most frequently occurring words, 396 spelling–sound correspondence rules, and no rule to tell you which one to apply! Morris, the exponent of phonics, spells out its problems in detail. Yet, she maintains, English orthography is highly patterned. Even the irregular spellings tend to fall into patterns. Her system is, she says, economic in teaching and learning time and encourages rapid progress to independence in reading and spelling. Her major claim is that the system is based on sound linguistics and helps children with the fundamental task of internalising a model of English spelling.

This is a sound goal. But what she does *not* do is suggest that her system is based on sound *learning* theory. In terms of linguistics it may be sophisticated, but in terms of psychology it tends to regard children as empty vessels to be filled, rather than as constructive problem-solvers. Sounding out the letters is always a schooled routine for children and it doesn't come naturally to them.

Nevertheless, the approach does supply something children need. As Adams, Frith and Bryant all suggest, children need to be *taught* the alphabetic principle about letter–sound correspondences, even if not as their initial introduction to reading. In addition to supplying sounding out routines, it feeds into their self-teaching processes in two ways at least. Firstly, it establishes a mental habit of attending to all the letters of a word in sequence, and secondly, it meshes with analogical processes of word-attack, helping to refine the recognition units.

ALL THE LETTERS IN SEQUENCE

Adams (1990) says:

> The reading process is driven by the visual recognition of individual letters in familiar ordered sequence and is critically supported by the translation of those strings of letters into their phonological correspondences. (page 237)

This may seem, at first glance, to be making a claim for teaching traditional phonics. But it isn't really a claim for phonics at all – or not 'first and fast' anyway. The emphasis on visual recognition of spelling strings or chunks points more to orthographic processes. The phonological processes are here operating in terms of chunks, not by synthetic phonics working on the individual letters. The question is, how do orthographic chunks become unitised? Analogy is one route, but phonics teaching may well – and in an unexpected way – provide another.

Adams (page 275ff) discusses an American study of First Grade children by Juel and Roper/Schneider (1985) on the comparative effects of two different basal reading schemes. All the children underwent regular tightly-scripted phonics lessons but the two schemes provided different levels of script-related repetition and emphasis on phonic decodability.

The children whose scheme complemented the phonics teaching better with relevant practice became better and more flexible in their reading skills, and their learning depended on how often a particular spelling pattern (or chunk) had appeared in *different* words. Still more provocative, Adams notes, was the differential pattern showing that these children were far more successful at reading spelling–sound correspondences they had *not* explicitly been taught. It seemed that they had developed a different mental approach towards decoding – they seemed to have generalised the alphabetic principle as a strategy to develop on their own.

Intriguingly, the phonics teaching did not seem to have much effect *unless* supplemented by reading materials conducive to practising and developing the phonic strategies. Juel and Roper/ Schneider conclude:

> The types of words which appear in beginning reading texts may well exert a more powerful influence in shaping children's word identification strategies than the method of reading instruction. (page 279)

It seems that the children did not gain so much from synthetic phonics routines as from chunking letters into orthographic recognition units and applying a generalised phonic strategy to new situations. Here is an instance of children learning more than they were actually being taught – but they wouldn't have managed without being taught in the first place.

In part, what children are learning in traditional phonics and the application of the alphabetic principle is a mental approach: both a habit of attending to all the letters in their sequence and a perceptual orientation to the phonological patterns of spelling in which spelling chunks take priority over letter-by-letter recoding. Such a strategy meshes with existing strategies and gives them a more detailed and systematic focus.

The learning process involved in the children's self-teaching is the spontaneous process of abstraction and generalisation from varied instances of spelling patterns met in practice. As Adams (1990) says:

> In time, as the commonalities among such patterns overwrite each other, their overlap emerges with a strength that is greater than that which can be owed to any one of the individual patterns from which it has grown. (page 211)

Instruction may provide abstract rules like 'the silent e rule' or 'when two vowels go walking, the first does the talking' but, to make sense, such rules have to be employed in regulated and varied practice. What children learn from such phonically regulated experience is *not* primarily the package of explicit phonics correspondence rules, but rather a much more implicit set of spelling-to-sound patterns built up inductively in practice.

CONCLUSIONS

The work of Ellis (1991) touches on the range of phonological issues we have been discussing. He studied a cohort of children during their first three years of reading instruction (from five to eight years old). Initially, they were tested over an array of abilities and then their progress was tracked. At the end of the study certain children were deemed to have specific reading difficulties because their reading abilities were poor (depressed) relative to their intelligence scores. When these children's initial test performances were re-examined, it became clear that there was a specific pattern of initial weakness that was associated with later difficulties. The findings were very much in accord with other studies. These children showed a deficit in rhyming tasks, in segmentation skills (identifying constituent sounds in words), in short-term auditory memory (for example, in immediate recall of a string of digits they have heard) and in naming (for example, deciding whether *G* and *g* are the same letter): that is, in the whole array of phonological skills. His conclusion was that these phonological skills play a large part in successful learning to read.

During these first three years of learning to read, the children's reading skills changed rapidly from an initial array of separate skills to a more unified, 'holistic' pattern of word recognition. At age six years, phonemic awareness and short-term auditory memory were most strongly associated with reading skill. At age seven years, analytic visual-perceptual skills (for example, seeing frequent and meaningful letter combinations as unitised 'chunks'), learning new sound–symbol associations (correspondence rules), and sound blending were the skills most closely associated with successful reading. Reading had become a multi-faceted ability, tapping a wide range of underlying skills from language comprehension to registering the visual order of letters. Further, the successful readers employed a variety of different strategies for merging these skills according to the challenges of different reading situations.

Along the developmental line of progress, the different skills interacted reciprocally with each other in different ways. In the pre-reading phase, phonological skills assisted in the children's acquisition of letter knowledge, and this, together with short-term auditory memory, helped the initial development of reading. In the reading phase, it was reading that helped further develop the acquisition of phonological skills, in particular, phonemic discrimination. And these skills helped further develop short-term memory performance. Spelling was consistently the best predictor of reading achievement, and spelling development depended on alphabetic and graphophonic skills. Altogether, then, the story was one of interactive processes in changing patterns of mutual facilitation within the developing system.

So what are we to conclude from all this? In many ways, phonological processes play a crucial role in organising our visual perception of print into meaningful patterns and chunks. Analogical inference draws attention to the spelling chunks associated with onsets and rimes. Traditional phonics and phonic spelling help by drawing phonological attention to every letter in sequence. These processes facilitate the learning of visual recognition units (spelling 'chunks' from digraphs up to whole words) which are the foundation of orthographic reading. It is to the development of orthographic processes we turn in the next chapter.

CHAPTER 6

ORTHOGRAPHIC PROCESSING

THE AIM OF THIS CHAPTER

The orthographic phase in reading development is the one in which we identify words directly from their spellings. This becomes the dominant process in most children towards the upper end of primary level, but it has been developing throughout the primary years, building on the child's phonological and alphabetic knowledge. Since spellings are a matter of sequences and relationships between letters, what we are looking at in the orthographic phase is the development of the identification and recognition of spelling patterns.

Alphabetic strategies in both writing and reading have the effect of directing attention to all the letters in their sequence. At the same time, the phonological patterns in words focus visual attention on the corresponding spelling sequences. Orthographic processing and effective adult reading depend upon internalising the spelling patterns so identified.

In this chapter we will first consider the visual processes of scanning print and identifying letters and words, then go on to look at the developmental processes of learning spelling patterns as orthographic recognition units.

VISUAL PROCESSING

Orthographic processing is a function of the visual processing system – but it is a very specialised function. It has its own rules of procedure for dealing with print, all of which need to be learned. These include the identification of letters and the directional scanning of print.

To take the question of letters first, John Downing (1979) points out that:

> ...the problem of identifying the objects b and d is that these letters contradict most of the child's previous experience of object identification – that is that an object remains the same object in spite of differences in its orientation... A chair is still a chair no matter what direction it faces...'
>
> *Reprinted in Clark, M.M. (1985),* page 48

But with letters it is different. You need to mind your 'p's and 'q's. New constraints have to be learned.

Perceiving letters is an act of interpreting what we see. In learning the letters of the alphabet, we learn which details are significant for discrimination. For example, we have to learn the 'G', 'g' and 'g' are the same letter but that 'n' and 'u' are different letters. Reception children, however, tend to think that letters are different depending upon what colour they are printed in, how big they are, how thick or thin the pen-strokes are. In teaching the alphabet, teachers need to establish which visual features are significant, and which are not. Perception needs to be educated to what is relevant for reading. Speed and accuracy in letter identification are essential for reading proficiency and development.

As with identifying letters, so with eye-movements in looking at print: new constraints have to be learned. A chair is still a chair, no matter which part of it you look at first. The order in which we scan its parts does not matter – and the same is true for logographic word recognition. But with reading proper it is different. The serial order of the letters and the words is of the essence. We have to learn the discipline of directionality. This is because we have to transform the visual (spatial) display on the page into the temporal sequence of language, one sound after another, one word after another.

As Marie Clay (1991) illustrates, there is plenty of scope for errors in learning directionality. Unless we are careful, children may make the wrong hypotheses about how they are meant to scan a page of print. The teacher needs to be alert to children's modes of operation. When reading aloud to children, she should point at the words she is reading to demonstrate the routine.

Clay strongly recommends that children should be asked to finger-point as they are reading, not only so that the teacher can monitor the child, but so the child has externalised support (like finger-counting for sums) in controlling her gaze and establishing the correct habits.

So far, then, we have sought to emphasise the importance of automatic letter recognition and left-to-right scanning of print, taking each letter and word in turn. But in practice, readers don't scan print quite like this. We need now to consider what the skilled adult reader actually does when reading, in order to realise what it is that the child has to learn. To do this, we will follow the process of reading from the bottom up: that is, from the printed word on the page to its identification in the Meaning Processor.

EYE-MOVEMENT IN THE FLUENT READER

In looking at anything, our eyes move, then stop, then move and stop again. The eye doesn't seem to notice much while in motion. These movements and stops are called saccades and fixations. During a fixation an image falls on the retina of the eye, and the part of the image falling on the central part of the retina, the fovea, is seen with greatest clarity. This is because the fovea is the area most tightly packed with nerve endings, giving the highest visual resolution. On the whole, peripheral vision ('out of the corner of the eye') is more sensitive to movement than to detail. In looking at any object our eyes range over it, fixating here and there, and our mental image of what it looks like overall is built up from all the different fixations.

In reading, we need to attend to the detail of print in its due sequence. Our saccades and fixations have to be disciplined to the line of the print and the patterning of the words and letters so that we put the right images together in the right order. This matter of sequencing the images correctly can be problematic for young children. For more experienced readers, knowledge of what *ought* to be there can help.

The study of eye movements using laser monitoring equipment is quite sophisticated. It shows that, in looking at print, on average the eye moves about eight letter spaces from fixation to fixation. There is a tendency not to fixate on very short words (often the function words, for example, *of*, *the*) and to fixate somewhere to the left of centre of longer words (probably content words). The eye resolves more letters on the right-hand side of the fixation point than on the left-hand side, three letters or more to the left, and twice as many to the right. This asymmetry is probably a consequence of learning left-to-right scanning. It appears that peripheral vision tends to control where the next fixation occurs, using peripheral perception of word lengths as a guide to probably-rewarding fixation points. The pattern of fixations along a line of print might go like this:

    +   +   +   +

In reading, we attend to the detail of print.

Allowing for the spread of letter resolution either side of a fixation point (creating 'text windows' of about 18 characters according to some recent research), virtually all the letters will have been visually resolved, and many of them twice over as a result of the overlap between different fixations. As a result, there are no perceptual gaps.

The duration of fixations is partly determined by the progress achieved in the analysis of the last two or three fixations, and also by word length. In continuous text there is a tendency to dwell upon the words that carry most meaning in context. Time taken doing this seems to be a matter of processing the overall meaning, rather than a matter of word identification as such. Young children and poor readers fixate more frequently and their fixations are of greater duration than fluent readers. Feedback from processing controls eye-movement.

One significant finding is that about 10 per cent of all eye movements are *backwards* along the line, as if checking back on the text. This suggests that in some way the words are being put into store for ordering and review before being processed for meaning; and it confirms that our scanning is in some way motivated by a search for meaningful information.

To summarise, studies of eye movements indicate that fluent readers pay attention not only to nearly all the individual words in the text that they are reading – skipping only a small proportion of function words – but they also visually resolve practically all of the letters in each word. These findings about attention to detail tend to contradict the widely credited view of Goodman, who has interpreted the saccadic movement of the eyes as indicating that not all words are actually 'read', with the reader needing to fill in perceptual gaps by contextually inspired guesses.

PROCESSING PRINT: LETTER RECOGNITION

Visual information from a number of fixations is integrated, allowing for visual overlaps and the effects of backward saccades, to retain the coherence and serial order of the information. In this way, visual processing produces manageable chunks of information to pass up the processing system.

The letters are processed according to their graphic features and their position in the letter-string. Any given feature may activate a number of possible letter identifications, but an identification is inhibited by incompatible features. These features include curves, horizontal bars, tails and so on. Thus, although 'n' and 'h' have many features in common, the ascender on the 'h' inhibits its identification as 'n', and the horizontal bar across 'e' inhibits its identification as 'c'. Between these processes of letter activation and inhibition, a unique letter identification is made.

Since a number of letters can be resolved visually at the same time, normally we don't identify letters one at a time but in 'eyefuls', still taking their sequence into account. As long ago as 1885, Cattell showed that fluent readers can identify whole words as quickly and as accurately as single letters or digits, and that whole phrases can be identified as quickly and easily as strings of three or four unrelated letters or digits. This is possible because, for the fluent reader, letter identification processes in familiar letter-strings mutually reinforce and support each other.

English spelling, while peculiar, is not entirely irregular. Certain letter sequences are not possible or are highly unlikely, while others are very likely to occur. Thus, the sequence *dr-* is a very likely sequence, but *dn-* is very much less likely (though it occurs in *midnight*). Reading experience establishes statistically-weighted connections between letters according to the frequency of their occurring together in spelling patterns. As a consequence, each letter will prime the recognition of other associated letters according to the strength of their connections.

Adams (1990) discusses the example of the word 'the', one of the ten most frequently-occurring words in print. The letters 't' and 'h' are highly likely to occur together as 'th' so the appearance of either of them primes the system for recognising the other. If they are both together, they each prime the recognition of the other. This mutual reinforcement makes the system just as 'th'-sensitive as it is isolatedly 't'- or 'h'-sensitive. Furthermore, all consonants are quite likely to be followed by a vowel, and 'e' is the most frequent vowel. So, by extension, the system will be equally 'the'-sensitive.

This effect of mutual reinforcement has far-reaching ramifications. These associations accelerate the identification of familiar words and familiar spelling patterns in unfamiliar words. The way that the sequences of letters in frequently encountered spelling patterns become bound together as perceptual chunks promotes what is effectively an automatised recognition system.

WORD IDENTIFICATION

One widely accepted theory of word identification postulates the existence of a mental dictionary or lexicon (see for example, Harris and Coltheart 1986). We met this concept in Chapter 2 when we referred to 'templates' to which ongoing perceptions are matched. The associative spelling patterns deriving from the 'serial probabilities' of particular letter sequences can be seen as the basis of these 'templates'. The processes within the mental dictionary work in the same sort of way as at the letter recognition level – by activation and inhibition. Certain letters or spelling sequences in certain positions activate a set of potential candidate word templates, for example, all the words beginning with 'pr-'. The same process applies to all the other letters in the letter-string. At the same time, they each inhibit incompatible candidate words. The process, then is a matter of matching the input, now at an abstract level of representation, with an abstract spelling-level entry in the mental dictionary.

A different theoretical model for word identification, the 'parallel distributed processing model', discussed by Mark Seidenberg and James McClelland (1989), dispenses with the notion of a mental dictionary and links orthographic, phonological and semantic aspects of word identification. It is the model employed by Adams when discussing the identification of the word 'the', referred to above. Computer learning studies based on this model are remarkable in the way they match empirical 'real-life' studies of children's learning. They demonstrate an inductive self-teaching system that relates frequencies of letter associations with phonological inputs. It learns to recognise frequently encountered words, whether their spellings are regular or irregular, and it also develops means of coping with new and unfamiliar words by applying the spelling-to-pronunciation patterns it has discovered for itself. One impressive result is that the self-teaching process proved self-correcting. This was shown in the way it coped with a few incorrect inputs it had been given by accident during its 'training'. For example, it was told that 'JAYS' was pronounced /jAs/, but, when given JAYS to 'pronounce', it output /jAz/. Seidenberg and McClelland (1989) observe 'These self-corrections were based on knowledge derived from exposure to related words, such as DAYS' (page 532).

Another interesting feature that emerges (interesting in

relation to Goswami and Bryant's work) is that rimes are highly significant. The priming effect of rimes that rhyme affected performance on new words. For example, exposure to *mint* facilitated performance on *tint*; but *pint* had interfering effects. *Tent* gave some help, but not as much as *mint*. This is because the key problem is the vowel sound, and *tent* doesn't address this. All this is very reminiscent of Goswami's work in her onset and rime 'clue-word' tests discussed in the previous chapter.

The effect of rimes is only one effect, however. Seidenberg and McClelland talk of the wider range of regularity effects as 'a conspiracy among known words'. Similarity of spellings and pronunciations produce overlapping, mutually beneficial effects.

This theoretical model replaces the notion of *access* to a mental dictionary with the notion of *activation* of different types of information. However, as Perfetti (1992) indicates, it is possible to reconcile the major mechanisms of this theory with the concept of a mental dictionary.

Overall, then, the model suggests that learning to read is a matter of the construction of an evolving network of associations between pronunciations and spelling patterns as they are encountered in reading experience. Because English spelling is so complicated, no simple decoding rules are likely to work (viz., the problems with phonics). But a simple *learning* mechanism can work: the strength of letter associations encodes the regularities in the input. Such a mechanism is appropriate where, as in English, the regularities are statistical and probabilistic, not absolute. Its critical characteristics include the ability to recognise familiar words, induce regularities to apply to new words, and yet be capable of learning infrequent irregular and exception words.

CHUNKING ORTHOGRAPHIC RECOGNITION UNITS

This theory about statistically-weighted associations between letters explains both word recognition and our capacity to employ spelling patterns at the sub-word level. Orthographic development means, among other things, the development of spelling recognition units within words. Since processing capacity is limited, our ability to deal efficiently and swiftly with input depends upon our ability to deal with it in 'chunks' rather than a letter at a time.

While the theory proposes that the chunks are discovered in processing the input material, the nature of the input is critical, as the work of Juel and Roper/Schneider (discussed in the previous chapter) suggests. They found that the nature of the reading material *and* the nature of the explicit instruction *and* the way these were related seemed to be important. What we, as teachers, draw attention to, and what procedures we encourage in the children, are significant. The input material needs to be phonological and the orthographic information associated in a way that facilitates the development of chunking.

WHAT KIND OF CHUNKS MIGHT WE BE DEALING WITH?

Initial sounds seem to be phonologically salient, as the traditional game of 'I-spy' and the teaching strategy of giving initial-sound prompts testify. Bryant and Bradley (1985), and then Goswami and Bryant (1990), have drawn particular attention to the salience of rimes. Through the processes of learning by analogy (discussed in the previous chapter), the spelling patterns associated with intrasyllabic units become salient recognition units. Such units are reinforced by frequency associations between letters. Seidenberg and McClelland (1989) remark that their model corroborates the common assumption that rimes are relevant to word naming:

> The end of words turn out to be salient because of the properties of written English; the pronunciations of vowels are more influenced by the following letters than by the preceding ones. The learning algorithm picks up these regularities... (page 544)

The spellings of rimes in general tend to be more reliable guides to pronunciation than their component letters are, considered individually. Thus, -ing is a much more reliable guide to pronunciation than its letters, considered separately, as to how it should be pronounced within, for example, ling. Learning by analogy, together with serial probabilities, helps to establish certain orthographic recognition units. Onsets create similar effects to those of rime, unitising consonant blends. Goswami's more recent work has suggested how both onset-vowel combinations and vowel digraphs may become recognition units.

Adams (1990) draws attention to another phonological principle at work, based not this time upon intrasyllabic units but upon the syllable itself. The syllable is an auditory perceptual unit but, even before this, it is a function of speech production. Because written English is alphabetic, and therefore follows the patterns of speech, every written syllable has to include a vowel. Since there are so few written vowels, the frequency with which any particular consonant occurs just before or just after any particular vowel must be quite high. That is to say, each consonant is strongly associated with every vowel. As Adams says, 'Each vowel must pull its surrounding consonants towards itself...' (page 121). This effect is so powerful that even a highly probable consonant pairing such as dr, straddling the syllabic boundary in 'midriff', is pulled apart by the vowel-power in each of the two syllables in the word. In general, then, the effect of this vowel-power is to make the written syllable a tightly-associated letter pattern. At the same time, in many polysyllabic words, highly infrequent letter sequences may straddle syllabic boundaries. Such pairings may tend to push the syllables apart. Thus, the unlikely dn pairing tends to push the syllables apart in 'midnight'.

We turn now to semantic considerations. Frith (1985), in her discussion of the orthographic phase, says: 'The orthographic units ideally coincide with morphemes' (page 306). She argues that the orthographic strategy is distinguished from the logographic by being analytic in a systematic way and by being 'non-visual'. By 'non-visual' she means that it is not dominated by striking visual details, but by learned associations between letters which form internally represented abstract letter-strings. Such strings, as we have seen, may be unitised upon the basis of phonological analogy, syllabic centring or simply upon statistical frequency of occurrence. However, she doesn't discuss these possibilities.

Her emphasis on morphemes appears to be an emphasis on meaning. If the characteristic of orthographic reading is direct access from spelling to meaning, then it makes sense to suggest that ideally the reader should process print directly into meaning-unitised chunks. She suggests that these morphemic units constitute:

> ...a limited set that... can be used to create by recombination an almost unlimited number of words.
> (page 306)

However, when she discusses the course of development from one stage to another, she suggests that certain components of older strategies may be retained because they enhance the new, developing strategies:

> For the orthographic strategy it is easy to imagine that there must be a merging of instant recognition and piecemeal analytical skills, each of which is assumed to be predominant at an earlier stage. (page 309)

It seems even more plausible to suppose that at least syllabic chunking, which will very often coincide with morphemes, will be retained. And in certain circumstances it would seem that onset, onset-vowel combinations and whole syllables all carry semantic potential, as in ps-, psy-, psych-. In the case of inflections (as in 'talked'), it could be that the morphological divide between the stem and the inflected ending is reinforced by the unitisation of each.

It would seem, then, that any teaching that encourages alertness to phonological or morphological structures must contribute to the establishment of a more flexible and comprehensive range of orthographic recognition units.

THE ORTHOGRAPHIC SIGHT VOCABULARY

Linnea Ehri (1991) argues that the development of the orthographic sight vocabulary is the most important aspect of the reading process. In order to read effectively (that is, with speed and comprehension) most words need to be read as sight words, virtually instantaneously. As adults we read nearly all words as sight words. With children, more than 80 per cent of words need to be read as sight words if reading is to be fluent enough for comprehension. This is because the alternative strategies are too unreliable or too slow.

It would be wrong, however, to assume that sight words are read by logographic means, using arbitrary and partial cues. Adams (1990) has shown that in adult reading virtually all the letters in a word are processed incredibly rapidly. This does not mean that they are each individually identified, but that rapid global identification of a word depends on its letters being all there, present and correct, contributing to the relevant recognition units. In terms of the mental dictionary, this means that the information stored in the orthographic template for recognising words is information about letters and spelling patterns.

In discussing whole-word recognition learning, Ehri draws a distinction between three stages or phases. In Ehri (1991) and Ehri (1992), she uses slightly different terminology. I combine the two versions here:

> Stage 1: Logographic, i.e, pre-phonetic, employing partial visual cues.
> Stage 2: Semi-phonetic, employing partial *letter* cues leading to partial graphophonic cues.
> Stage 3: 'Cipher' reading, i.e, phonetic sight-reading of the word as a unitised whole, including spelling, pronunciation and meaning.

As we saw when discussing logograms, pre-phonetic reading is relatively inefficient because it doesn't discriminate between visually similar words (for example, *yellow/smaller*). Semi-phonetic reading is more efficient in that it uses phonic cues (especially initial letter sounds) but, because it is incomplete, it doesn't distinguish between similar words – as, for example, between 'parcel', 'packet', and so on, in 'She tore open the p_____ .' In phonetic ('cipher') reading the complete spelling of a word is recognised as the visual symbol for its pronunciation.

But how does this 'cipher' reading develop from semi-phonetic reading? Ehri (1992) argues that establishing sight word reading is a matter of establishing systematic visual–phonological connections between complete spellings and pronunciations in memory. The learning is word-specific, not a matter of translation or correspondence rules, and pronunciation is accessed directly from the printed form, not by way of recoding. Her theory is congruent with Seidenberg and McClelland's, in that she argues for a unitary system to account for the reading of regular, irregular and pseudo-words. It is a matter of building up whole spellings from smaller recognition units.

'Cipher' reading bypasses phonological recoding but nevertheless involves phonological processes. The connection from the visual (orthographic) processes links spellings to pronunciations rather than directly to meanings. That is to say, reading processes are parasitic on phonological access to meaning – so no wonder we hear what we read in the mind's ear! This route is originally established by phonetic recoding processes, though the recoding element is bypassed once the learning is established. Figure 1 (opposite) represents the processes of learning to 'cipher' read and 'cipher' reading itself. It can usefully be compared with Figures 4 and 5 in Chapter 3, pages 52 and 54.

At first (arrow 1) orthographic information has to be recoded to establish a pronunciation. The pronunciation then accesses meaning. But soon a direct link (arrow 2) is established that allows the orthographic information to stimulate the pronunciation directly. The primary access to meaning in 'cipher' or orthographic reading, even if no longer involving

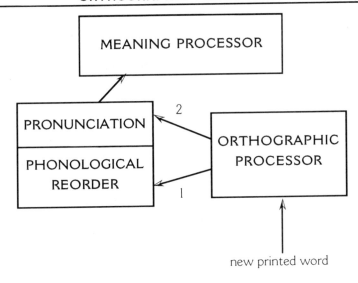

Figure 1

Developing 'cipher' reading.

phonological recoding, involves the phonological process of pronunciation as a staging post in accessing meaning. As Ehri says:

> The spelling itself is used to enter lexical memory and locate the word's pronunciation... No intermediate translation is required... Recoding rules may be used to set up this route. However, once the word has been recoded several times, the rule and the translation and the phonological matching routines drop out to be supplanted by specific connections linking the spelling directly to its pronunciation in memory. (page 120)

What Ehri is offering here is a model of how orthographic sight reading comes about, tutored by phonological recoding. As Perfetti (1992) argues, such 'word recognition is holistic in appearance and non-holistic in reality' (page 146). It depends upon remembered systematic connections between spelling recognition units and pronunciation and, in this way, is consistent with the global model of orthographic processing that we have been developing.

Altogether, then, we begin to see a general view of the way phonological processes are involved in establishing the sight vocabulary of orthographic reading. From this, we see why easy letter identification, habits of reading all the letters in sequence, recoding skills, and plenty of reading practice are so important. We can also see that what the learner ultimately has to learn are not explicit correspondence rules but implicit statistical associations that operate at an automatic and unconscious level. The outcome of these processes is the identification of words in the text. How we make sense of these words is the subject of the next two chapters. But before we leave the issue of word identification, we should perhaps consider more fully some of the implications of these ideas for teaching.

IMPLICATIONS FOR TEACHING

Ehri (1992) spells out the implications of her views for teaching. Clearly, letter knowledge and rudimentary phonemic segmentation skills are essential as they are the two best predictors of subsequent success. Among other things, she recommends pictorial mnemonics (pictograms) to help teach letter–sound associations. She encourages the use of invented spelling to teach phonemic segmentation and believes that the words children have to learn should have phonetic cues for them to latch on to. Children start using such cues before they learn to recode, even using them before they have learned all the letters of the alphabet.

Concurring with Frith and Bryant among others, Ehri maintains that children need explicit instruction and assistance to move on from phonetic cue reading to recoding, because this development is not entirely spontaneous. She argues, however, that neither traditional phonics teaching nor whole-word teaching (like look-and-say) is ideal. Whole-word teaching doesn't give sufficient letter and phonetic segmentation practice; and phonics, while good at some things, may create precocious but dead-end recoding routines if it moves on too fast for phonetic cue reading to establish habits of perceptual chunking. Children stuck in mechanical phonic recoding routines are not equipped to bypass the recoding stage and move on to 'cipher' reading.

The implications for teaching, then, relate to the learning of the letters of the alphabet, to establishing reading and writing routines that involve full serial processing of the letters in words, to exploring phonological spelling patterns using a controlled vocabulary and to encouraging lots of reading practice. If Smith's dictum is anywhere true that children learn to read by reading, it is in the development of orthographic sight reading skills based on the implicit internalisation of English spelling patterns.

SUMMARY

To summarise, the key elements for effective orthographic development are:

✦ rapid and accurate letter identification;

✦ habitual processing of all the letters in a word in their serial order;

✦ learning to relate spelling sequences with sound sequences in words, leading to phonological recoding;

✦ the establishment of orthographic recognition units for identifying familiar whole words and for building up unfamiliar words from familiar spelling patterns;

✦ lots of experience of reading, in the first instance with plenty of repetition of words that exhibit regular or frequent spelling patterns.

CHAPTER 7

THE QUEST FOR MEANING: CONTEXT AND SYNTAX

THE AIM OF THIS CHAPTER

The bottom-up processes we have looked at in the last two chapters were concerned with the identification of words. Identifying words comes first. But we don't simply read words, we read words in sentences as parts of acts of communication of some kind. Top-down processes are concerned with the ways we construct meaning from the words we read. In this chapter we will start to look at the contribution of context and, in particular, of syntax (the grammatical rules that govern word order in sentences) to comprehension.

THE LEXICO-GRAMMATICAL SYSTEM

The child comes to reading with an existing knowledge of the language system. This means that, to some extent, she knows the words and the grammar of the language. This has been called the child's *lexico-grammatical system* (Halliday 1975). Knowledge of the words means that she has a system of connected and related word meanings which are part of the conceptual structuring of her knowledge and experience of the world. Thus, if she knows the word 'dog', she will know how the meaning of the word relates to other words like 'cat', 'pet', 'animal', 'bark', 'puppy', and so on. She will also have mental images of dogs, memories of experiences of dogs, including dogs in picture books, stories and on television, and information about dogs, for example what they like to eat, how they like to chase sticks, and so on. If she reads about dogs, all this information is available to her and plays its part in the sense that she makes of what she reads. So when she reads Eric Hill's 'Spot' books, this knowledge prepares her for making sense of the stories. The stories access, activate, select from, add to and reorganise this knowledge to create the specific meanings of the narrative.

In order to create these meanings, to make sense of the words, the reader not only needs to know the meanings of the words, she also needs to know how grammar organises word meanings into sentence meanings. Children are not born with a knowledge of grammar – they go on learning the specifics of grammar throughout their primary years and beyond, and may never learn the entire grammar of their mother tongue. But they are born with a remarkable ability to construct rules for themselves that progressively approximate to standard grammar. My daughter, for example, aged 3.2 years, displaying a plaster on her knee, announced proudly, 'It much bleeded, lotter than if you'd been cut in half!' She had clearly learned how to put word meanings together to construct her own personal meaning, and in doing so she was using grammatical rules. But clearly the rules she was using were not quite the standard rules!

Incomplete grammatical knowledge affects children's reading performances. For example, Katrina (aged 7.0) is still not secure on past tenses: she reads, '...he cooked the next lot of worms he caught' as '...he cooked the next lot of worms he catched'. She repeats 'catched' three times, as if not quite sure about it, but finally settles for it. It seems her current knowledge of grammar has priority over the graphophonic evidence!

Complex grammar is difficult to master. There may be two contributory factors to this difficulty: one is that the rules may be difficult to learn and apply in the first place; the other is that, in actual situations, the processing system may be overstretched, having too much to cope with all at once. For children starting to read, one of the problems is that they are still in the process of acquiring the grammar of the language, and the grammar of writing is more complex than the grammar of speech. Nevertheless, syntax provides one of the strongest contextual supports to the beginning reader.

CONTEXT PROCESSING

The processor model presented in Chapter 3 indicates the contribution of various elements to the Context Processor. The lexico-grammatical system is represented by syntax and semantics. The other elements of prior knowledge indicated as contributing to the context are experience of life and of literature. These elements together create the context in terms of which the text can be interpreted and a meaning constructed.

The concept of context, and its contribution to the process of making sense of text, is central to the viewpoints of Ken Goodman and Frank Smith, two major figures in the world of reading whom we have mentioned in earlier chapters. They have been highly influential in establishing the dominance of 'whole language approaches' in current practices. One of the most widely used reading schemes firmly announces its commitment to the 'whole language approach' thus:

> The sequence of learning underlying the approach of the Oxford Reading Tree may be expressed as follows:
>
> Meaning → Sentences → Words/letters
>
> (the sequence underlying most vocabulary-controlled schemes is: Letters/words → Sentences → Meaning)...
>
> ...Although young children cannot 'understand' separate letters or isolated words on a page, they can understand and retain a simple story told in natural-sounding language patterns. (*Oxford Reading Tree Teacher's Guide* 1986)

This statement expresses many of the core beliefs of the 'whole language approach'.

In Chapter 1, we discussed Ken Goodman's theories on the three systems of information that the reader employs in reading – graphophonics, syntax and semantics. What he means by the terms 'syntax' and 'semantics' includes the elements we showed as contributing to the Context Processor. In this and the following chapter the various aspects of context will be considered in turn, indicating how they contribute to comprehension.

SYNTAX

We have a very strong drive to make grammatical sense of words when they appear in sequences. For example, we readily parse (work out the grammar of) telescoped headlines to make sense of them. For example:

Death Riddle Suicide Claim

Shuttle buses hope for town

To make sense of the second headline, for instance, we don't read 'hope' as a verb! It is only where we are given a highly specified construction and we cannot play with grammatical possibilities and ambiguities that we are obliged to reject certain word-strings as meaningless, for example, 'Tell me new he went'.

The power of our grammatical drive is also illustrated in cloze procedures like the following, where the task is to fill in the blanks:

There was such a clattering and rasping, and clinking _____ gold, and grinding of _____, as he rushed _____ of the cave that he _____ they were both _____ him. He daren't look back. He rushed to the _____ ... (*The Voyage of the Dawn Treader* 1965)

Even if you can't always be sure of the exact word to fill each blank, you can be sure what part of speech (noun, verb, adjective, preposition, pronoun, and so on) is required.

There is plenty of evidence to support the view that syntactic awareness is important in learning to read. Performance and training in oral cloze procedures relate positively to early reading achievement (Tunmer and Hoover 1992). Yet the way in which syntactic awareness helps reading is not simply by facilitating psycholinguistic guessing but, rather, to adapt a diagram from Tunmer and Hoover (1992), the situation is more like this:

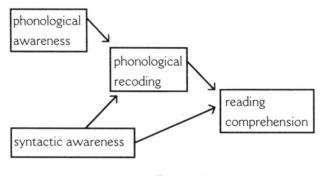

Figure 1

Syntactic awareness works in combination with phonological awareness in facilitating phonological recoding skills. And both phonological recoding and syntactic awareness contribute directly to reading comprehension. Syntactic awareness contributes to the development of phonological recoding largely by helping in the identification of words, thus permitting graphophonic learning from experience. It contributes to reading comprehension by parsing and keeping track of the relationships of meanings in sentences.

Syntax, as the system of grammatical rules that specifies word order in phrases and sentences, organises meaning. The following two sentences are only different from each other because of their word order:

Jenny kissed James.

James kissed Jenny.

The words are the same, but the meanings are different because the word order is different. The relevant rules about word order here are: the grammatical subject of the sentence precedes the verb, and the object of the verb follows it. The syntax, coded in the word order, tells us who is the 'doer', agent or actor, and who is the 'done to', recipient of action or acted upon, in each case.

Children come to reading with a basic, though implicit and incomplete, knowledge of English grammar. Manipulating grammar remains difficult for them. Nearly half of seven-year-olds and a quarter of eight-year-olds cannot sort out jumbled sentences like 'The log jumped Jack over.' Yet Ken Goodman (1993), among many others, has observed that when children 'miscue' (that is, make mistakes) in reading a word and substitute another word, they very rarely substitute a word that doesn't fit grammatically. Goodman cites this example from seven-year-old Patricia (the actual text is followed by the child's version):

One day a man left his village to tend to his field of corn.

One day a man left his valley to tender to his flower.

He remarks, 'These real-word substitutions keep their grammatical functions but don't quite make sense....' (page 58). One might question whether Patricia knew 'to tender' is a real verb, but the general point is valid: keeping to the syntax appears to be a very strong constraint, even stronger than making sense.

There are some aspects of syntax which children are not likely to be familiar with when they first come to reading. There are, for example, some literary turns of phrase in 'book language' which they may find problematic. For example, Ros Fisher (1992) cites a miscue by Emma, aged 7.9 years, when reading a poem from *Please Mrs. Butler* (Allan Ahlberg 1984). For:

We have to go out at playtime.

she reads:

We have got to go out at playtime.

'Got to' is much more natural and colloquial.

Goodman (1993) cites some examples where a child named Janice is misled by unfamiliar syntax, all involving prepositions:

'I will go over there' becomes 'I will go over the...' (apparently expecting the phrase to continue)

'Something came down!' becomes 'Something came down...' (apparently expecting the phrase to continue)

'And on she went for a walk' becomes 'And on the...' (again, expecting the preposition to be followed by a noun phrase)

In each case Janice is led to expect something that isn't then confirmed by the text. Her experience of prepositions seems to have led her to expect prepositional phrases along the following lines:

over the road

down the chimney

on the way.

Her predictions are proved wrong. Her encounter here with different prepositional structures demonstrates Harris and Coltheart's (1986) contention that language is 'essentially unpredictable' (page 170). Prepositions are not predictably always followed by noun phrases. For example, they are sometimes parts of phrasal verbs, such as 'go on' or 'put up with'.

However, this is not the moral Goodman draws from these examples. He says:

It's obvious that simple reliance on phonics can't solve Janice's problems with these unusual syntactic patterns. In controlling the words in this "story", the authors and editors have created clumsy, unpredictable grammar. Her miscues show her trying to find a structure that will allow her to make sense of the reading. The text has certainly contributed to her miscues... (pages 56–7)

If by 'simple reliance on phonics' Goodman means paying attention to the written text, it seems obvious to me that a simple reliance on the written text would help solve her problems! As it is, however, Goodman blames the 'clumsy, unpredictable grammar', but the grammar is not wrong, it is simply unpredictable. Maybe the problem is not the grammar, but over-reliance on prediction. How is a reader to learn anything new about grammar unless she reads what is actually there, rather than what she expects? As Goodman says on another occasion:

> ...to be effective – that is, to make sense of print – readers must use phonic information along with meaning and grammar cues. (page 60)

Nevertheless, in relation to Janice's efforts, Goodman has a point. Children who are learning to read should not be outfaced by challenges. If they are to acquire the ability to cross-check between top-down and bottom-up processes, and then self-correct as necessary, they need texts they can cope with at the three levels of decoding the print, parsing the grammar and comprehending the meaning, all at the same time. If the potent support of syntax is to be available, the syntax the child encounters should be largely familiar, if not entirely predictable.

Most contemporary reading schemes set great store by natural language patterns and familiar sentence structures in order to offer children the best possible chance of making correct predictions. By 'natural language', people generally mean structures and vocabulary that are close to the language that children spontaneously produce. Katherine Perera (1993) discusses the linguistic features of 'good books' for beginning readers:

> There is... a case to be made for the use of the kind of sentence patterns that children are likely to hear, and to use in their own speech. This case rests on the evidence from research by people like Rose-Marie Weber (1970) that beginning readers who are reading aloud say what they expect to find rather than necessarily what is printed. This suggests that familiar language patterns will lead to more successful prediction and, therefore, to a greater sense of achievement. (page 96)

Weber's findings, cited here, certainly correspond with Goodman's sentiments about predictable grammar. But Perera goes on to argue that the structures of written language are different from 'natural' spoken language. Consequently, children need at some point to be introduced to these written structures. Nevertheless, she says that the language they encounter, whether familiar or more literary:

> ...should be the language that people really use, rather than a kind of language, sometimes known as "readerese", that occurs exclusively in books written to teach children to read. (page 96)

'Natural language' is generally seen as following this basic active indicative sentence structure:

subject – verb – (object) – (adverbial)

(NB The brackets represent optional elements.)

As examples of this structure, let's look at some sentences from *Castle Adventure* (Oxford Reading Tree).

subject	verb	object	adverbial
The witch	opened	the door.	
Gran	pushed	the witch.	
Chip	took	the witch's keys.	
They	ran		out of the room.
She	put	a net	over the witch.
The witch couldn't get out.			
(NB 'Get out' is a phrasal verb incorporating its own adverbial.)			

Perera says that such unrelieved sequences of short sentences sound rather stilted and unnatural. While recognising that the general pattern of short sentences probably makes the young reader's task easier, Perera regards variety of sentence length as sounding more natural. More naturally varied language is less predictable than the short, simple structures illustrated above, but provides opportunities for encountering and learning new structures and usages.

It is difficult to keep aspects of syntax and semantics separate from each other. There is a semantic aspect to the form of such basic sentences as the examples given above that helps understanding. The grammatical subjects of the sentences we have been looking at are 'the witch', 'Gran', 'Chip', 'they' (Chip & co) and 'she' (Gran). They are all the active 'doers', agents or actors, who perform the actions. The verbs represent the actions they undertake. This means we can interpret the basic sentence form in the following terms:

	subject	verb	object
	actor	action	acted-upon
i.e.	somebody	does	something

This basic active sentence form of 'somebody doing something' tends to promote narrative, and stringing such sentences together can readily extend the narrative – as *Castle Adventure* demonstrates. Such narrative sentence structures are easy for children to understand, but grammatical structures that differ from this basic form can be difficult for young children to cope with. Let us consider just two sorts of different sentences: passive and complex sentences.

The nature of a passive sentence is counter-intuitive: the grammatical subject is not the doer of the action, but the done-to. For example:

subject	verb	object	adverbial
Bill	was given	a book	by John.

In terms of action, John is the doer of the deed, though Bill is the grammatical subject. Young children, however, tend to try to apply an active grammatical model when processing sentences and this can lead to difficulties. They take longer to comprehend passive than active sentences because processing them is harder. Slobin (1966) showed that reversible passives are harder to comprehend than non-reversible passives. A reversible passive is one where the role of doer and done-to could be interchanged and still produce a sensible sentence, for example, 'The cat is being chased by the dog.' A non-reversible passive, where an interchange of roles is not semantically possible, is easier to comprehend, for example, 'The flowers are being watered by the girl.' This was just as easy to comprehend as the active sentence 'The girl is watering the flowers.'

These examples suggest that *plausibility of meaning*, as well as grammatical structure, contribute to the successful comprehension of sentences. As Carlotta Smith (1970) argued, interpreting sentences may not depend so much upon syntax as upon semantics. Certainly, in practice, the two are thoroughly intertwined.

The tendency to want to activise sentences can result in some striking miscues. For example, in the following from the BBC video *Teaching Reading*, sentence (i) was read by an upper primary child as sentence (ii):

(i) It needs people to agree with one another that...

(ii) And people need to agree with one another that...

The effect of this is to simplify the syntax without changing the meaning – a 'good' miscue.

A possible explanation for the problems children have with passives also applies to complex grammar: it creates a processing overload – with simply too much to sort out all at once. This factor has many, many ramifications in relation to reading development. While syntax can be a great support in reading by permitting certain kinds of prediction, syntactic processing of complex and compound sentences with limited working memory capacity can itself create problems.

Because of the limitations upon working memory, syntactic processing is not foolproof. It tends to work by a rule-of-thumb – the rule of proximity that says, relate the words that are nearest to each other. For example, seven- to eight-year-olds find problems with sentences like:

The girl standing beside the lady had a blue dress.

Many young children will say that the lady was wearing a blue dress. It is as if the rule of proximity, together with limited memory capacity, constrained the children to construe the last six words of the sentence as a grammatical structure in its own right:

>...the lady had a blue dress.

Similarly, Margaret Donaldson (1978) cites Reid's finding that 36 per cent of seven- to eight-year-olds misconstrued the sentence:

>Tom walked in front of Dick and carried a flag.

They said that Dick was carrying the flag. The problem here seems to be inexperience in dealing with compound sentences and ellipsis (leaving out unnecessary words to avoid repetition). The word 'Tom' is the subject of both verbs and does not need to be repeated, but a certain memory span is needed to remember 'Tom' when 'Dick' is much closer.

One example should suffice to illustrate how a simple ellipsis can cause a young reader problems. Emma (7.9 years old) is reading these lines from Allan Ahlberg *Please Mrs. Butler* (Fisher 1992):

>The teachers can sit in the staffroom
>And have a cosy chat...

But what she says is:

>The teachers can sit in the staffroom
>And we have a cosy chat...

She is constrained, apparently by syntax, to provide a subject for the verb 'have'. What is more, she gets it wrong. If she said *they* instead of *we*, we would deem it a 'good' miscue: the meaning would have remained the same. But in the event, her failure to understand the grammar has led to a failure to understand the meaning.

TEXTUAL COHESION

The limitations of working memory can also create problems with textual cohesion. 'Cohesion' refers to the verbal links between sentences that mark the coherent thread of meaning running through them. For example, in the following passage, the pronoun 'it' links the meaning of the two sentences:

There is a dragon in the house.

It hides in the bathroom.

(*Sunshine Spirals: The Dragon* 1993)

Pronouns are typical cohesive devices in texts, and yet children can very easily lose track of them. It can be hard to follow what they refer back to because they demand that the child carries over information from one sentence to the next. This is one reason why nouns tend to be repeated from sentence to sentence in some early reading books, rather than being replaced by pronouns, as would happen in more 'natural-sounding' discourse.

Eleanor Anderson (1992), discussing cohesion at length, cites this example from a very simple information text intended for young children:

Then it bites it with its fangs and poisons it.

In trying to make the words simple, the references become complicated. Cohesion, intended to highlight links of meaning, can itself create problems where children have limited retention and understanding of what has gone before. Yet following the chain of references indicated by pronouns is essential for making coherent sense of texts.

SUMMARY

What are we to conclude from this very restricted survey of the role of syntax and the problems it poses for children in making sense of text?

✦ Syntax is a powerful constraint on prediction and comprehension.

✦ Children's grasp of syntax is limited as a result of three interconnected factors: limited experience of all the grammatical structures of the language; a tendency to try to make sentences fit the most basic structures; and limited working memory capacity.

✦ Syntax normally works hand-in-glove with semantics, and is more laboured when required to work on its own in construing sentences.

On its own, even in ideal conditions, syntax can only successfully predict one word in four and, even then, the words are typically frequent function words, not content words. Of course, it does not work on its own, but in combination with other processes, like phonological awareness, phonological recoding and semantics. Even so, prediction is not the main value of syntax. Its value is twofold: firstly, in causally contributing to the development of phonological recoding processes; and secondly, in contributing to reading success by guiding the comprehension of sentences.

CHAPTER 8

THE QUEST FOR MEANING: SEMANTICS AND COMPREHENSION

THE AIM OF THIS CHAPTER

This chapter is about comprehension and the way meaning is constructed from text. 'Semantics' is the study of meanings, and in this chapter we will consider the way word meanings build up into sentence and discourse meanings.

WORDS AND MEANINGS

Earlier chapters discussed word meanings at some length and looked at how they relate word and world knowledge. We said that not only do we have some kind of mental representation of a word (auditory and orthographic) that allows us to identify it as a word we know, but we also have a concept or schema of its meaning in relation to other meanings and, where appropriate, some kind of mental image. Thus, we said, with the word 'dog', we do not only have a concept of a dog but also a whole range of connections and experiences associated with dogs and a number of mental images we can call upon. It is possible to think of our word knowledge as consisting of, among other things, dictionary-like definitions or *denotations* such as 'man = human + male + adult', and *connotations*, a set of meanings that may or may not apply in a particular case. Specific contexts activate appropriate selections from this range of meanings. For example, Kipling's 'If' concludes: '...you'll be a Man, my son.' Clearly in this context Kipling is not concerned with the denotative meaning of 'man' (human + male + adult), but with a particular range of connotations that the poem has been establishing (independence of mind, integrity, moral courage and so on).

Word meanings are, then, to some extent, a collection of potentials from which a selection is made. We are largely unaware of how different connotations and images are activated by different contexts. For example, we don't have to think twice to understand the different contextual meanings of the common words in the following:

the river running by	first go
time running out	go to town
a running nose	go to sleep
gun running	go for gold

Each meaning is clear and specific in its context.

This account of word meanings applies to *content* words, and also to some *function* words. Consider the words in the following:

A yellow kite in the sky.

The content words are the two nouns (*kite*, *sky*) and the adjective *yellow*, the function words are *a*, *in* and *the*. The function words have no meaning except what they tell us about how to understand the content words and their relationships. Nevertheless, even function words are affected by context. For example, consider the use of 'in' in the following:

in the sky	in tears
in the morning	in favour
in time	indoors

A very high proportion of the words in a text are function words. McNally and Murray's (1968) work on key words shows that a quarter of all reading consists of 12 function words, and that half of all reading consists of only 100 words, most of which are function words. Meaning, however, depends disproportionately on the content words – for example, we get more meaning from 'yellow kite sky' (it sounds almost like a haiku!) than from 'a in the'. The content words provide concepts and images to work on and, within the syntax of the phrase or sentence, the function words help us organise and adjust their meanings in relation to each other.

CONSTRUCTING THE MEANING
OF A SENTENCE

Constructing the meaning of a sentence is not just a matter of adding up the meanings of the content words. Without the context of a sentence as a syntactic arrangement of content and function words, we do not know how to organise the meanings, nor what particular meanings to organise. It is this fact that leads Frank Smith (1985) to say:

> Rather than the words giving meaning to the sentences, it
> looks as if the sentences are giving meaning to the words.
> (page 71)

Until we know the meaning of the sentence, we cannot know which meaning of a word will fit. He goes further, and argues that we cannot even be sure of the syntax until we have understood the meaning, because syntax is so often ambiguous. For example, let us consider this sentence from 'The Babysitters' (*Sunshine Spirals* 1993):

> The giraffe looked after the baby crocodile.

It would be possible to interpret this sentence in various ways. We could imagine it in the following contexts:

> The baby crocodile looked first. The giraffe looked after the
> baby crocodile. Then the lion wanted a turn.

or:

> The baby crocodile packed his bags and set out on the road
> for the big city. The giraffe looked after the baby crocodile.
> 'I do hope he will be all right,' she sighed.

But in point of fact, the story begins:

> "I am going out," said the crocodile to her baby. "The
> babysitters will look after you." The giraffe looked after the
> baby crocodile.

In this context there should be no ambiguity about the syntax or meaning. The verb is the phrasal verb 'to look after'.

Nevertheless, Smith's statement, given above, about words and sentences is misleading – it is only half the story. It is, after all, the words that give meaning to the sentences that give meaning to the words. The construction of meaning is not a simple linear process. The true story is not:

word meanings → sentence meaning (traditional view)

nor:

sentence meaning → word meanings (whole-language view)

but rather:

→ word meanings
sentence meaning ← (interactionist view)

We could call this 'the semantic circle'. But it is a circle that has a starting-point – as Marilyn Jager Adams (1990) points out, it is the words on the page that cause the whole reading process to 'kick in'. The 'semantic circle' is another way of talking about top-down and bottom-up interaction where word identifications and context effects mutually reinforce each other in arriving at a meaning (see Chapter 3). Bottom-up processes identify the words. The words are held in the short-term working memory while syntactically and semantically interpreted. The developing sense of the whole sentence then specifies the sense or meaning of the words in context.

There is no way we can know what the meaning of a sentence is except by attending to the words. But the meanings we attribute as we process the sentence are provisional and open to amendment. The context may have primed us for particular meanings – for example, 'babysitters' will have primed us for interpreting 'look after' as a unit (the equivalent of 'take care of'). It is likely, as a result of contextual priming, that the meanings we attribute provisionally to ambiguous words (and most of the commonest words are ambiguous) will not require revision. Other meaning potentials are there, however, ready to be exploited if the construction of overall sentence meaning demands it. Thus we may construe the phrase 'sailing boats' as a noun phrase, with *sailing* fulfilling an adjectival function. But compare the following two sentences:

Sailing boats are nice.

Sailing boats is nice.

In the first case, the whole sentence confirms the adjectival role of *sailing*; but in the second, the verb demands that we re-parse the grammar of the sentence. *Sailing* now has a noun function as the grammatical subject of the sentence. Not only do we have to revise the grammar, we also have to revise the appropriate sense of *nice* to suit the context. In the first case, it might have the sense of 'attractive', but in the second case it has the sense of 'enjoyable'. Both grammar and word meanings are determined while the words are held in the working memory.

THE SOURCE(S) OF MEANING

Frank Smith (1985) says that within the reading process, 'Everywhere we look for sense...' (page 73). In the quest for meaning, one source is our drive to look for sense – that is, to make our internalised mental model of the world (what Smith calls 'the theory of the world' that we each have in our heads) as complete and coherent as possible. So when we read a sentence, what we are looking for is a schema or meaning that fits in with our established mental model or 'theory of the world'. Comprehending meaning is about fitting things in with, filling out and extending our conceptual structures. Our sense of meaning is our sense of how things fit together to make a coherent whole. That is the reason why, in 'The Babysitters' example given on page 126, we took 'look after' to mean 'take care of' and not anything else – we made the meanings all fit together.

In another sense, the source of meaning is our prior knowledge or theory of the world and this enables us to make sense of new sentences and their meanings, by ascribing existing meanings to the parts and fitting them together in familiar or, at least, plausible conceptual structures. But we have to make sense *of something* so, in yet another sense, the source of meaning is the sentence itself. Because we can 'learn the new' (Chall's phrase, 1983) from reading, the source of meaning must in part lie within the sentences.

THE 'GIVEN' AND THE 'NEW'

One way of considering how we 'learn the new' from sentences involves examining the sentence linguistically in terms of the 'given' and the 'new'. The 'given' is the part of the information that the speaker, or writer, assumes to be shared with the recipient, and the 'new' is the information about the topic to be transmitted.

Typically, a sentence consists of subject and predicate (where the predicate consists of verb + (object)). According to pragmatics (the semantics of communicative contexts), typically the grammatical subject of a sentence tells us the topic, which is the 'given', and the predicate gives us the information about the topic, the 'new' or comment on the topic. Thus, in pragmatics, the form of the sentence is:

subject	predicate (i.e. verb [+ object])
given	new
or topic	comment

'Topicalisation' can easily be identified in certain habits of speech, as shown in the examples below:

'Please, Miss. You know James, Miss? He keeps kissing us.'

'You know Granny? She says...'

The rhetorical question in each of these examples is not a real request for information, but an act of topicalisation – 'I'm going to tell you something about James/Granny'. This is then followed up with the substantive information. But even within the sentence communicating the substantive information we can distinguish topic/given and comment/new:

(topic or 'given')	(comment or 'new')
He	keeps kissing us.
She	says...

Coherent texts develop by adding progressively to the 'new'. There is a tendency for each sentence in turn to treat the 'new' of the previous sentence as the 'given' which it treats as its starting off point, as can be seen in the following two examples:

(i) You know James, Miss? He keeps kissing us.

(ii) Several people have recognised how important analogies may be to children who are learning to read. The most outstanding initial work on the topic was done by George Marsh and his colleagues. It was they who pointed out...

(Goswami and Bryant 1990, page 65)

Clearly comprehension must depend not only upon understanding each sentence but upon being able to follow the chain of meanings through the sentences, typically indicated by the cohesive device of using pronouns to refer back to what has previously been said. In (i) we wouldn't know who 'he' was without the previous sentence naming James, nor in (ii) would we know who 'they' were in the third sentence without the comment of the second sentence.

The 'given/new' link between the first two sentences in passage (ii) is a little more complicated. The comment of the first sentence (transformed now into the word 'topic' itself!) is only a subordinate part of the complex noun phrase that forms the topic of the second sentence. The second sentence is passive, permitting reference to the 'doers' (Marsh *et al.*) to be part of the comment, ready to be topicalised in the third sentence. Such sophisticated writing, dense in texture, complex in structure and flexible in focus, demands a sophisticated reader!

COHERENCE AND 'LEARNING THE NEW'

The coherence of a text (depending as it does on textual cohesion) requires that the 'new' constantly becomes the 'given' so that the discourse can move forward. This is true of narrative and even more so with non-chronological writing.

Carol Feldman (1987) sees striking parallels between the way the 'given' and the 'new' work in discourse and the way cognitive thinking works. She argues that thinking operates upon objects of thought (concepts, schemas). These very objects of thought, however, were themselves originally acts of thinking and have undergone a transformation from being a 'new' activity to becoming a 'given' something to think about.

According to Feldman, the parallel between thinking and language has two aspects: both distinguish between 'given' and 'new'; and in both, the 'new' of one step can be transformed into the 'given' of the next step.

We can see this in considering the following sequence:

> The elephant sneezed. This brought the house down.

In the second sentence, the pronoun 'this' refers to the whole meaning of the first sentence. A meaning is constructed in one sentence, and it is then referred to as an established object of thought in the next. Here we see a congruence between the linguistic processing of 'given' and 'new' and development in mental operations. This congruence doesn't just facilitate the relationship between language and thinking: the linguistic forms are the embodiment of the thinking process moving on. In a continuous discourse each sentence creates a building-block of meaning that is the foundation for the construction of the meaning of the next sentence. Feldman argues that this process 'may help explain one of the ways in which language is instrumental in shaping thought' (page 145).

This process is a major aspect of comprehension. It constitutes a step-by-step reconstruction of the meanings that the writer incorporated in the text.

INFERENCE

There is a further major element in comprehension. So far we have been concerned with 'reading the lines', but we also have to consider 'reading between the lines'. We need to consider the place of inference in comprehension.

Making inferences is a sophisticated comprehension skill. It involves not only understanding the explicit text but filling in the gaps in the text with extra-textual information based on our knowledge of the world and what is plausible. For most purposes, this takes place automatically at an unconscious level in terms of assumptions we make.

Jane Oakhill and Alan Garnham (1988) cite and comment on the following passage from a children's story:

> Jane was invited to Jack's birthday party.
> She wondered if he would like a kite.
> She went to her room and shook her piggy bank.
> It made no sound. (pages 21–2)

They argue that this story can only be understood against the background of a particular culture with particular social practices, for example, practices of celebrating children's birthdays. They say that to understand the second sentence correctly, 'you have to realise that Jane did not simply wonder if Jack would like a kite, she was thinking about buying him one for his birthday' (page 22). Similarly, we infer her motive for going to her room and shaking her piggy bank because we understand the situation and we know what piggy banks are for. The last sentence has to be understood as meaning she had no money to buy the present. A great deal of what we *ought* to understand in the story is implicit, rather than explicit.

The meaning we construct from a story is ultimately a mental schema, not a memory of the wording of the story. We tend to remember both explicit and implicit meanings integrated into a whole. The more work we have invested in making inferences, the better we tend to remember things – perhaps because the whole, so constructed, is more coherent.

Making inferences about what is implicit in the text, while apparently instantaneous, is measurably slower by milliseconds than processing explicit information. The more explicit the text, the easier it is to comprehend. Inferring is a higher order activity, so it is not surprising that younger readers are less good at it – indeed, as Tunmer and Hoover (1992) remind us, young children often fail to notice when they don't understand. They are often not alert to inconsistencies and gaps in information in texts. Two factors may account for this: their relatively immature decoding skills and their relative lack of experience of life. In due course, greater speed and efficiency in bottom-up processing will free processing capacity for dealing with such higher order activities as inferring and interrogating the text. And more experience of the world and of texts will give them models of meaning and plausibility to incorporate into the interpretations they construct. These higher order activities can, and should, be encouraged by discussion of stories during the process of reading.

In discussing what they call 'pragmatic awareness', Tunmer and Hoover deal with how meaning builds up in continuous discourse from sentence to sentence. Pragmatic awareness deals with coherence and cohesion in discourse, together with inferences, prior knowledge, knowledge of the preceding text and of the situational context. It involves the reader monitoring her own comprehension of sentences and working on that comprehension to build up the larger context of meanings.

There is, they claim, no evidence that pragmatic awareness makes any contribution to reading development in the earliest stages. Rather, the situation seems to be that reading comprehension is the product of decoding skills and listening comprehension. They maintain that reading achievement influences listening comprehension which, in turn, influences reading comprehension. It is as if reading skills enhance self-monitoring abilities in comprehension and the purposeful control of attention, which are key requirements for 'self-teaching' processes. Failure to achieve this self-monitoring ability creates a cascade of further functional failures, including motivational problems. Their findings highlight the importance of teachers aiming to develop children's comprehension skills orally, knowing this will help develop self-monitoring abilities and reading comprehension.

OUR KNOWLEDGE AND EXPERIENCE OF THE WORLD

Comprehension involves using what we know already to make sense of the new information coming our way. Sometimes this is a matter of fitting the new in with what we already know and sometimes it is a matter of using what we know to make inferences that go beyond what we are explicitly being told.

We cannot easily keep syntactic and semantic issues conceptually separate, nor can we keep them separate from questions of knowledge and experience of the world. In actual reading, these three elements work totally together, and we only separate them in our discussion here in order to make their contributions conceptually clear. For example, Judith Greene (1986) cites the experience of seeing a poster saying:

> The Police live at the Albert Hall

How do we know we are supposed to read 'live' as an adjective, not as a verb? The most straightforward syntactic strategy (following the active sentence model) is to treat 'live' as a verb, but the meaning would then not square with what we know to be plausible. So we try a different parsing (and pronunciation) of 'live'. When a plausible syntactic interpretation squares with a plausible semantic interpretation, the quest for meaning has probably achieved its goal. But note, our notions of semantic plausibility depend on all kinds of knowledge from outside the text.

We only interpret the word 'live' in the example above as an adjective, and not as a verb, because we bring to the text our knowledge that 'The Police' is (was) the name of a pop group and that the Albert Hall is a famous venue for concerts. We also know that the Albert Hall is not a hall of residence of any kind and that police officers do not usually live together! We are aware of the social function of posters for advertising events, not making statements about people's living arrangements. That is, our comprehension depends upon our general knowledge of the world. Our knowledge of linguistic contexts also contributes to our interpretation: we know that 'live' in the context of music refers to a performance in person, rather than to a recording. Such social knowledge, like the knowledge we have about how birthdays are celebrated, provides us with models of social behaviour in specific situations. Employing the same metaphor that gives us social 'roles', such models have been called 'scripts'. Our social knowledge is organised in 'scripts' which can be readily accessed to assist comprehension.

UNDERSTANDING STORIES

Writers write on the assumption that their readers share with them not only the language but also certain information and expectations about the world. This shared information enables the reader to make plausible inferences and interpretations from the text.

A novel is perhaps one of the most complex of text types in terms of exploiting our capacities for making assumptions and inferences based on shared knowledge and frames of reference. Much of the meaning of a novel we bring to it ourselves from our own experiences — experiences both of life and of other novels. Our sense of the fullness of an imagined world depends upon our having filled it out with our own inferences and assumptions.

Our reading of novels is also influenced by our learned expectations or schemas relating to stories, that is, our knowledge of 'story grammar'. Stories require characters and settings in time and place but, most importantly, they require a challenge or problem that is resolved through action. For example, Katherine Perera (1984) cites a news story by a six-year-old boy:

Our dog got lost. Dad found him.

This story has the essential elements of story, even if some of the elements are implicit:

✦ an initial situation marked by stability — here, a home situation implicit in 'our dog';

✦ a problem or challenge, upsetting the initial stability — the loss of the dog;

✦ significant action — in the quest as dad searches for the dog;

✦ success and resolution, with the restoration of stability — the dog is found.

Such a plot can be amplified endlessly, in terms of characters and settings, with the action divided into many episodes, partially successful or failing, and so on. But there is enough here to constitute a plot with the emotional themes of loss and recovery.

One of the things that children learn to look for in reading is the sense of an ending that resolves the issues the story raises. Comprehension of a story is largely a matter of recognising the issues of plot and theme, interrogating the story in relation to them and recognising when the questions have been answered. Thus story schemas and, as we have seen, scripts can provide frames of reference to help structure-developing interpretations.

The useful questions that a teacher can ask in the course of a story are concerned with elucidating these issues and themes and interrogating the story. Wondering what happens next is essential, since this provides the suspense that keeps you reading. The teacher can help children by asking questions about what is happening on each page to encourage inference-making, questions about what the issues are, what the children want to know about and what questions they want the next page to answer. Interrogating the text in this kind of way is a vital comprehension skill and re-reading the story in the light of the ending develops new perceptions and a new savouring of meanings. Reading for comprehension involves, on the smaller scale of graphophonics and syntax, attention to the wording of the text and, on the larger scale, attention to the widest range of meanings to build up the schema of the story.

SUMMARY

To summarise what we have been saying about the quest for meaning, we can look at the processes in terms of differences between good and poor comprehenders:

✦ Good comprehenders perceive the task of reading as understanding the meaning of the text, whereas poor comprehenders perceive the task of reading as simply to decode the text.

✦ Good comprehenders are more sensitive to context for constructing meaning than poor comprehenders, but are not dependent on context for purposes of decoding.

✦ Good comprehenders identify words more rapidly than poor comprehenders, thus freeing working memory for higher order processes like parsing the syntax and integrating information from neighbouring clauses or sentences.

✦ Good comprehenders exploit syntax to help chunk the text into meaningful units, while poor comprehenders tend to read word-by-word. Since the *sense* of a word depends on its place in a meaningful unit, word-by-word readers, however accurate, are at a disadvantage.

✦ Good comprehenders construct running schemas as they read that both link up the meanings of sentences, and also fill in gaps in the explicit meaning by inference and the use of existing knowledge. Because they have constructed more complex and coherent schemas, their recall of text meanings is greater.

Comprehension, then, goes beyond the explicit in the text. It involves two main elements: *integrating* the meanings of the different sentences and the inferences drawn from reading between the lines; and *constructing* an appropriate mental model or schema, incorporating both new and established knowledge in a coherent whole.

CHAPTER 9

PUTTING IT TOGETHER: CHILDREN'S READING STRATEGIES

THE AIM OF THIS CHAPTER

In this chapter we will try to pull together all the theoretical ideas discussed so far by applying them in a discussion about the developing strategies that children employ in trying to make sense of print. If we have a model of how children generally develop their reading skills and we are able to identify the strategies that any particular child is using, then we are in a strong position to help that child move forward towards more effective reading processes.

First we will recapitulate the major themes of development, then look in more detail at miscue analysis as a window on to children's reading strategies and, finally, review the progression of strategic developments.

A RECAPITULATION OF THE THEORETICAL PERSPECTIVE

The overall theory put forward in this book seeks to show how top-down and bottom-up processes work in concert. Bottom-up processing deals with processing the print on the page – its contribution to meaning is in identifying words through graphophonic processes. Top-down processing deals with context – both the syntax of the ongoing sentence and the semantics of the words in the context of developing discourse meanings. Bringing the bottom-up and top-down contributions together, the Meaning Processor makes sense of the text in relation to the sentence, the discourse and the reader's whole body of knowledge, permitting comprehension to take place.

The bottom-up identification of printed words on the page is what causes the rest of the processes to kick in. At the heart of word-identification are the graphophonic processes of linking spoken-word knowledge with spellings. Learning to match the sounds within words with the visual patterns of spelling chunks eventually establishes orthographic recognition units that recode reliably into speech-sound patterns. These units are reinforced because they result from the experience not just of one word, but of many words sharing the same spelling sequences. For example, every time I read *light* and *right*, my ability to read the much less frequent *wight* is strengthened – or at least, re-confirmed.

What we observe in all this is the way that phonological processes tutor the development of orthographic processing. Orthographic reading is dependent on spelling recognition units based on the systematic spelling patterns of English, which are initially identified through, and continue to be linked with, their pronunciations.

So much, then, for our summary of bottom-up processes concerned with graphophonics. What of the top-down processes concerned with syntax and semantics?

Comprehension depends upon more than good word identification performance. Indeed, as Tunmer and Hoover (1992) argue, the following equation represents the basis of reading comprehension:

$$\frac{\text{decoding}}{\text{skills}} \times \frac{\text{listening}}{\text{comprehension}} = \frac{\text{reading}}{\text{comprehension}}$$

Reading comprehension clearly depends upon decoding skills in that if you cannot decode the text, you cannot comprehend it! But to take this further, it depends on general language comprehension skills, first developed in listening. As indicated by the equation given above, if either decoding skills or listening comprehension skills are deficient, then reading comprehension will be deficient.

Reading comprehension depends in part upon the phonological nature of the short-term working memory.

Ongoing, tentative syntactic constructions are re-evaluated in the light of the whole sentence, and the relevant senses of the words are selected in such a way as to maximise coherence of meaning within the sentence and general context.

Only when this is done can the meaning be transformed into a gist and dispatched to a longer term memory store. Meanwhile, the detail of the actual wording of the sentence slips out of the short-term working memory (which is now required for the next sentence) and is forgotten.

What we comprehend is more than the sum of all the gists. The gists become fused in our memory with inferences we make while reading. Many studies have shown that we don't remember the actual sentences we have read, but rather the sense we have made out of them, including the inferences we have drawn in the light of our previous knowledge and experience.

MISCUE ANALYSIS AND IDENTIFYING CHILDREN'S READING STRATEGIES

Miscue analysis, like Marie Clay's similar 'running record' technique, permits diagnostic interpretation of children's reading errors, giving us, in Ken Goodman's (1973) phrase, 'a window on to children's reading strategies'. In order to obtain miscues to analyse, the child has to be challenged with a text a little too difficult for her to cope with competently. Miscue analysts then interpret the miscues or errors and assume that the strategies that have been attempted reflect the pattern of strategies that have been employed successfully elsewhere in the reading. But this interpretation begs the question: how do we know that the strategies attempted unsuccessfully are the same as those used successfully for familiar words? The question of interpretation of miscue analysis is an important one to consider, but first we will examine the procedures involved.

Helen Arnold (1982) is keen to remind us that miscue analysis has two elements: the analysis designed to identify the strategies the reader is employing more or less effectively; and the comprehension element involving recall of the text at both the literal and the inferential levels. Since comprehension is what reading is all about, this second element can hardly be left out! We will start by looking at the relatively straightforward recall and comprehension element.

Goodman's criteria for assessing the retelling of the story that has been read operate in fairly broad terms – character analysis, events and their sequence of recall, plot and the underlying pattern of events and theme together with viewpoint and generalised attitudes. Helen Arnold recommends the use of multiple-choice question schedules, distinguishing between literal recall questions ('What colour was...?') and questions based on inferences ('How do you know that...?'). The aim is to test the overall schema of the story that the reader has constructed and retained.

With regard to the other element, miscue analysis on the text, the test procedure goes like this: a suitable passage is chosen and a copy is made of the text for the teacher to mark up. The child is given the text to read silently to herself before reading it aloud and preferably, the reading is tape-recorded because marking up can be quite a slow business.

The following is an excerpt from a marked up text. The reader was Kirsty (aged 7.0).

---

change-a   the
Merah Chaga made jokes about this fishing; but he did

not stop his brother. He thought, "If he can catch a
                     hi- ✓
few fish, it will give/us something to eat; and if he can

catch a few more, perhaps we can sell them, and that

will give us some money to buy clothes."
                      to/ be ca-/
   But Merah Silu did not seem/able)to catch any fish.
       that
Each day/he would go down to the river. He might

see a fish swimming about. But whenever he brought
      net   was
(in)his nets he found there were only worms inside.

The miscues marked up here are:

✦ Substitutions: indicated by writing the substituted word in above the corresponding word in the text – for example, 'Change-a' for 'Chaga', 'the' for 'this'.

✦ Omissions: indicated by ringing the omitted word(s) – for example, 'in' in the final line.

✦ Insertions: indicated by writing in the inserted word above an insertion mark – for example, 'that', following 'Each day...'

✦ Self-corrections: indicated by a tick after the miscue marking – for example, where Kirsty first read, 'it will give hi-', then stopped herself and re-read it correctly as, 'it will give us...'

✦ Repetitions: indicated by underlining once for each repetition – for example, where Kirsty repeated the words 'it will give...' as part of her self-correction, and where she repeated the 'when' part of whenever'.

✦ Hesitations: indicated by an oblique stroke – for example, Kirsty paused between trials in trying to cope with, 'did not seem able to catch...'

There are no examples in this excerpt of non-responses, reversals (of word order), phonic 'sounding out', nor teacher help, all of which may be marked up.

PROCEDURES FOR SCORING MISCUE ANALYSES

Once they have been coded, miscues need to be interpreted. However, not all the features recorded in miscue analysis are strictly miscues – hesitations, repetitions and self-corrections are not miscues (though they still need to be interpreted). Helen Arnold (1982) regards hesitations and repetitions more as indications of style than of strategy. Marie Clay (1991) might regard them as indications of developing carefulness, self-monitoring and inner control. In Kirsty's case, her hesitations seem to occur when she is trying to work something out, and her longer repetition seems to have been a matter of wanting to re-read the clause as a meaningful whole, which I would interpret as a mark of developing inner control, like the self-correction it accompanies.

Scoring genuine miscues is largely a matter of categorising errors as falling under one or other, or some combination, of the *graphophonic, syntactic* and *semantic* strategy headings. Arnold employs the graphic device of three overlapping circles, one to represent each of the three strategies, and then plotting the numbers of miscues in each category. She cites the example of Angus (aged 8.2) reading 'bodies' for 'boys', and codes this miscue within the overlap between all three categories, because there is evidence of some graphophonic 'reading work' (the first two and the last letters), some syntactic 'reading work' (both are plural nouns) and some semantic 'reading work' (it can be taken as a plausible, if odd, reference to the boys in the context). Below I give my plotting of Kirsty's miscues over the 256 word passage from which the excerpt is taken.

graphophonic 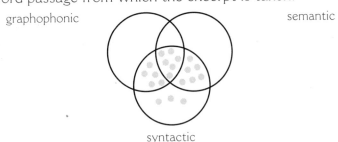 semantic

syntactic

From this display we can see that all Kirsty's miscues show her to be influenced to some degree by the constraints of syntax. Except for those miscues that show *only* the influence of syntax, all the others show multiple influences. A good proportion of these fall within the central, three-influence area, and as ideally we would wish a reader to use *all* available sources of information, this is an encouraging sign. She seems to be using all three strategies, though she could usefully be encouraged to apply graphophonic and semantic cues more fully.

As significant as this plotting of miscues is Kirsty's pattern of scores for the different categories in the whole passage: fifteen substitutions, six repetitions, three hesitations, two omissions, three insertions and six self-corrections. Her rate of self-correction indicates that she is self-monitoring and cross-checking her different sources of information, and it is possible to interpret most of her repetitions similarly, as self-checking strategies. One of her hesitations occurred before the name 'Sumatra' which she then pronounced in a phonically acceptable form, suggesting she had worked out the pronunciations graphophonically in her head. Her two omissions seem to result from syntactic problems – the 'seem able to' construction and the phrasal verb 'to bring in'. She appears to be unhappy about reading out something which is meaningless to her. Even her insertion of 'that', creating a non-sentence, probably results from her attempt to make sense of the rather literary usage of 'would' to indicate habitual action. She is more likely to have come across 'would' in constructions like, 'He said that he would...'. The pre-emptive insertion suggests that she is reading ahead of pronunciation, working out the meaning.

Her substitutions arise from a number of causes. Her pronunciation 'Change-a' for 'Chaga' suggests that she assimilated the name to the known word 'change', so her reading here is at best semi-phonetic. Her self-corrected miscue, reading 'hi-' for 'us' shows she is alert to the cohesive use of pronouns and was expecting the sentence to continue with the same subject. Some other substitutions seem to be a matter of 'naturalising' the language of the text – 'this' to 'the', 'were' to her native Yorkshire 'was'. In an earlier part of the passage, she substituted 'eldest' for 'elder', again supplying a more familiar and colloquial usage. All this suggests that her miscues are influenced strongly by her desire to make the text make sense in her own mind by naturalising it.

She had a struggle with the expression '...did not seem able to catch...'. This was the only occasion on which she seemed finally to give up on meaning. Perhaps, in inserting 'to' and 'be', she was influenced by the possible construction 'seem to be...'.

In the end, the impression she gave was not of having simplified the sentence by the omission of 'able', but of moving on with relief to the next phrase, which she gets right. One cannot be sure whether her problem was with decoding the word 'able' or with making sense of the syntax, but the latter seems more likely.

In contrast, Lee (aged 6.11), reading the same passage, managed this sentence without error or hesitation. Altogether he made very few miscues, with just four substitutions and six omissions. However, compared with Kirsty, Lee had only the most rudimentary grasp of the story, only being able to recall that there were some men catching fish! It is significant that his omissions included jumping a whole line of text on three occasions without appearing to notice that what he was reading didn't make any sense. One wonders whether he had no problems with reading the 'seem able to' construction, as others had, because he has no expectation that reading should make sense!

Clearly, finger pointing to keep track of the lines, and work on comprehension would benefit Lee. With Kirsty the situation is very different. She seems already to employ many of the strategies necessary for self-teaching, in that she is seeking meaning, self-monitoring and self-correcting her reading when sources of information do not match up. Despite her higher rate of miscues, she will gain from private reading, whereas Lee probably will not.

SELF-CORRECTION

According to Helen Arnold (1982), some miscues are 'good' or positive, others are negative. The grounds for determining 'goodness' (or not) is whether the version read makes reasonable sense, not whether it is accurate. However, it should be noted that, by definition, even 'good' miscues are indicative of failings.

For Arnold, self-corrections are 'good', except when they correct a 'good' miscue. Where Angus (8.2 years) reads 'socks and shoes' for 'shoes and socks' and then self-corrects, Arnold scores the self-correction as negative, an 'over-correction', because the miscue hadn't changed the meaning. However, it seems perverse to say self-correction is *not* positively 'good' in every case. As Marie Clay (1991) remarks:

> The child who learns to take self-correcting action because the sources of information do not match has made another big advance. (page 168)

Self-correction is important because it involves self-monitoring, which involves recognising a miscue and seeking more information to achieve a correct response. As such, Clay maintains, it 'may prove to be very important in explaining how the effective reader learns more about reading while reading' (page 301). The reading work involved in such problem solving 'has high tutorial value for the reader' (page 307).

INTERPRETING MISCUE ANALYSIS

The overall pattern of miscues gives guidance as to what sort of strategies the reader may need help in developing. However, interpreting the pattern of miscues raises important theoretical issues. For example, Ken Goodman (1993) discusses the case of Patricia (Second Grade) who stumbles badly on 'poor broken stalks', reading it as 'door barken sta-ul-ks'. For him, she represents over-reliance on phonic strategies as she 'diligently tries to sound out each word' (page 57), and he looks forward to the time when she 'will give herself permission to make sense of print as she reads' (page 60). Similarly, Helen Arnold (1982) concludes that Angus (aged 8.2), who showed many miscues in the area of graphophonic overlap but only two within the semantic area, did not exploit semantic context cues sufficiently. There is a tendency for miscue analysts to conclude that semantic strategies are being underexploited. This monotony of interpretation results from the underpinning 'whole-language' theory that children learn to read by top-down processes of semantic prediction.

An alternative interpretation might be that if shaky phonics is leading to miscues, the answer is not to depend more heavily on a different strategy but, rather, to improve the graphophonic processes. Semantic strategies should not be used to compensate for weak graphophonics. As Goodman (1993) himself says:

> To be efficient – that is, to make sense of print – readers must use phonic information along with meaning and grammar cues. (page 60)

The interactive model of the reading process presented in this book emphasises cross-checking and mutual support between the three sources of information. Semantic processes do not compensate for poor skills in other areas, but rather provide feedback on whether those processes are operating effectively. The model we are considering is not based on the assumption that the way forward for children is to develop better and better psycholinguistic guessing strategies but, rather, that the way forward is to develop better and better orthographic sight reading.

So, as Goodman (1993) claims, miscue analysis can provide a window on reading strategies. But what one sees through the window needs appropriate interpretation. Miscue analyses can provide valuable assessment information when viewed from an appropriate theoretical perspective. But, perhaps most important of all, experience of *doing* miscue analysis changes the teacher's attitude and approach forever to listening to children read. Instead of seeing it as a chore that you devote half your mind to while marking on the side, it becomes an enthralling diagnostic exploration.

PHASES AND READING STRATEGIES

Learning to read is a matter of co-ordinating skills and strategies of different kinds – graphophonic, syntactic and semantic – to tackle printed text. As Marie Clay (1991) says:

> The integration of skills cannot occur so long as the child is happily inventing text rather than reading it. (page 156)

But first, there have to be some skills to integrate.

THE EARLY STAGES

The child's first task with reading is to recognise that it is a matter of reading the words that are there on the page. At first the child conceives the task of reading a picture book as generating book-like speech based on the pictures. The critical first step towards reading is when the child recognises print as a distinct message-bearing part of the page and expects it to act as a label for the picture. Another critical step is achieved when she begins to relate specific graphic segments of the print on the page with sound segments of the spoken text. This would seem to be the crucial perception for reading development to begin. The link between specific sounds and specific marks creates a new potential for meaning – a world where things lock together in reliable relationships is a world the child can make sense of.

DEVELOPING STRATEGIES

The logographic phase is characterised by the rote-learning of words, identifying them from some aspect of their visual appearance. Gough *et al.* (1992) tell a tale of teaching four- and five-year-olds some words using flashcards. For each child one card was sullied by a thumb-print in the corner. In subsequent tests it was found that, in the case of the sullied cards, what the children had learned to identify was the thumb-print!

Yet the rote-learning is not mindless. Yetta Goodman (1990) tells a revealing tale:

> Quincy, aged four years, says as he looks at the word *Ivory* on a card which has had its logotype shape retained: "It says soap, but you know if you put a dot up here (he points to the *i*) that's in my name, and if you put a line down here (he points to the *o*) that's in my name, and this... this... (he is pointing to the *y*) this is... (Then he points to each finger on his left hand with one of the fingers on his right hand as he continues his analysis.) This is *q-u-i-n-c-y*... That's a *y*."
> (NB Ivory is a brand of soap) (page 138)

While his logographic association leads to his identifying *Ivory* as saying 'soap', his interest in his own name, and his ability to spell it, show him to be ripe for learning about the alphabet.

This first phase of 'reading' from partial cues is a critical step. Generally, the partial cue is a visual feature of the printed word. Gough *et al.* further record an experiment involving teaching children four-letter words (for example *lamb*, *duck*) using flashcards. The children were then asked to identify the words with only the first two, and then only the last two letters showing. They found that most children learned to recognise a cue in one half of a word and not the other, confirming the notion of partial cue learning. But at least these cues were related to letters!

DIRECTIONALITY

The next important step in learning to read is for the child to learn directionality, the left-to-right and top-to-bottom scanning of print. Marie Clay (1991) believes that:

> ...we have for too long underestimated the magnitude of this task and its particular relevance to subsequent success in learning to read. (page 39)

This is something the child can only learn from watching experienced readers who give a clue as to what they are doing. Directionality is not something the child can readily infer. There is no intrinsic reason why English should not be written and scanned right-to-left like Urdu or vertically downwards like traditional Chinese. The particular directionality of English is arbitrary and can only, therefore, be learned as a convention taken over from others. The adult who finger-points while reading and lets children watch her writing is giving the emergent reader an essential lesson. Writing, in particular, demonstrates the separateness and left-to-right sequencing of letters within words as well as the sequencing of words themselves.

CHILDREN'S SELF-GENERATED READING THEORIES

Even when the critical understandings of written-word/spoken-word relationships and directionality have been grasped, the child may only be at the logographic stage. Children tend to assume some kind of iconic relationship exists between a word and its meaning: just as the word 'children' denotes more children than 'child', so 'children' has more letters and is a bigger word. 'Elephant' is a big word because they are big animals. The relationship between 'mouse' and 'mice' might well be counter-intuitive to a child at this stage!

Yet at the same time, as Marie Clay (1991) records in an anecdote, a three-and-a-half-year-old, who wrote his name by making a capital 'M', asked his mother to write 'Devon/Seven'. Marie Clay remarks:

> As an observer, I wondered if he was asking for D-evon/S-even as though it were D+X and S+X which would have been an interesting analysis on his part... (page 30)

Apparently, the child had discovered rhyme and wanted to explore the relationship between the print versions of words and their sounds. It seems as though he wanted to explore the possibility of graphophonic, rather than merely logographic, theories about word forms. This anecdote is consistent with Goswami's (1994) contention that children entering school already have expectations about how orthography might work, based on their phonological knowledge about language.

Bryant and Bradley (1985), as we have seen, argue that children make the connection between rhymes and spelling patterns for themselves. Before they begin reading they have been inclined to form categories of words according to common onsets or rimes, so they are pre-sensitised to spotting common spelling sequences which represent a common sound. According to Goswami and Bryant (1990), this link enables them to make inferences about new words as soon as they begin to read, even if they aren't always very successful. Reading development is largely a matter of children, with growing experience, gradually becoming more skilful at this strategy and getting more of their inferences right.

At this point one of the signs of progress, according to Marie Clay (1991), is the slowing down of response to text, finger-pointing and studying the text to match up printed word with spoken word, perhaps even checking back to another page where a word was previously encountered. Response to text becomes a slow and deliberate word-by-word process, with self-correction playing an important part. Fluency is lost – but then, so is invention and paraphrase. The child is trying to bring her reading under the control of the print, and using all her resources to do so.

DEVELOPING INNER CONTROL

Marie Clay's (1991) book, subtitled *The Construction of Inner Control*, highlights the importance of self-correction at this stage of learning written–spoken word correspondences. Inner control is the control the child has over her own strategies. What is important, she says, is that:

> Most high progress readers can be noticed interrelating information from more than one level of information in print from their very first attempts to read, and they get better and better at doing this. (page 237)

Inner control is flexible control, cross-referencing between top-down and bottom-up processes. She doubts if there is any necessary sequence for developing the component processes, so long as they develop flexibly together. It seems to her that different teaching approaches cause children to develop their processes differently, and that the only danger is that children will rely too heavily on one strategy, rather than developing on a broad front across all the strategies and using them to complement each other.

So the first signs of inner control, evident in the early months of school experience, are a combining of directionality, close visual attention to words and matching spoken words to them slowly, deliberately and with self-corrections. During this time, both analogical inferences and the accumulation of grapheme–phoneme correspondences learned from writing begin to supply semi-phonetic cues to supplement the logographic sight vocabulary. Development takes the form of cultivating new strategies, getting better at existing strategies and meshing strategies as evidenced in self-correction. One of the main areas of development is in discovering things about the written code, in particular, the importance of small differences in spelling. In this way, the discrimination net becomes more discriminating.

At first, the child will tend to employ only one cueing strategy at a time, but towards the end of the first year of instruction, the child's miscues will show an increase in substitutions that show a meshing of strategies. The child who is attentive to print develops new ways of discovering cues for herself, and the more she reads, the more opportunities she has for doing so – so long as the reading material is sufficiently rich in instances. The problem-solving involved is its own reward.

At this stage, reading aloud helps the child in many ways. It assists word identification by accessing the phonological route very directly, it permits easy self-monitoring (and indeed, may be a necessary stage in developing internalised feedback systems) and it supports short-term auditory memory in assembling words from recognition units and sentences from words. In fact, its usefulness in enabling the teacher to monitor reading progress is, perhaps, its least important function!

In the first year of learning to read, Clay (1991) found that directionality and the expectation of meaningful and grammatical sentences developed early. Sound associations were not used overtly, presumably because children were still operating largely logographically. In the next year and a half or so (up to about seven-and-a-half years old), children acquired word-solving skills that enabled them to read new words, and they corrected themselves. During this period, graphophonic cueing rapidly gained in importance.

Miscue evidence, as we have suggested, does not tell us how children read the words they read successfully. These will tend to be familiar words readily recognised visually – which, at this stage, increasingly means graphophonically and, in the case of the commonest function words, orthographically. Overall, the progression of development is towards attention to the wording of the text, and this requires graphophonics to take the leading role until it is superseded by the orthographic processes that it has helped to foster.

SUMMARY

To summarise strategic progress, then, over the early years:

✦ The child comes to instruction using her spoken language experience and stock of past associations, including logograms, to help predict likely meanings.

✦ At some time during the first year of instruction visual perception begins to identify phonic cues but, for a long time, these are piecemeal and unreliable. However, directionality is established and this helps serial organisation and matching of visual cues with spoken words and sounds. Syntactic and semantic expectations, along with logographic and semi-phonetic cueing, are the dominant processes.

✦ A slowing down of response and careful word-by-word reading mark a change in orientation as the child focuses on the task of printed word identification.

✦ Alphabetic skills merge with existing skills to secure the priority of graphophonics in the reading process by the time the child is six- to seven-years-old. Graphophonic processes spontaneously give rise to orthographic processes as words become familiar.

✦ Inner control, correlating graphophonic, syntactic and semantic sources of information, results in reading becoming more completely subordinated to the printed text.

Growing inner control characterises reading development. How the mutually-enabling meshing of processes develops is very difficult to unravel, and is probably different for each child but to give undue emphasis to any one process at the expense of the others is misleading, and may lead to unbalanced teaching strategies. Margaret Meek's (1982) suggestion that the teacher has made herself unnecessary is evidence of just such an unbalanced view. It is to the necessity of teachers that we turn in the next chapter.

CHAPTER 10

THE TEACHER'S ROLE

THE AIM OF THIS CHAPTER

This chapter will discuss the teacher's role in the light of the theoretical viewpoint put forward in this book, considering in particular some of the practices and approaches the teacher might have in her repertoire. Though not an exhaustive account of 'how to teach reading', hopefully the discussion indicates how theory can be linked with and underpin practice. The final responsibility, however, lies with the teacher to use the insights and deploy the approaches and suggestions as she thinks appropriate.

The stages of developmental progress determine the general progression of teaching. Since children may start school with very different levels of attainment and find their way through these stages in different ways and at different rates, depending on background experience and innate propensities, the teacher has to be diagnostically alert to individual children's strategies and needs. Nevertheless, many games and activities, as well as storytime, lend themselves to group teaching and discussion and can be valuable to children at different stages.

What is important in all aspects of the teacher's repertoire is that her performance is underpinned by a clear idea of what she is aiming for and how it fits into the whole developmental process. As Marilyn Jager Adams (1990) says:

> It is not just eclecticism that makes a program of reading instruction effective; it is the way in which its pieces are fitted together to complement and support one another, always with full considerations of the needs and progress of the young readers with whom it will be used. (page 423)

THE TEACHER'S ROLE

The teacher's role in teaching reading has many facets. Ros Fisher (1992) describes the literacy teacher's role as a facilitator, a model, a manager and an assessor. We should perhaps also add the role of instructor to this list. After all, as Peter Bryant (1993) suggests:

> ...it is entirely up to teachers to remove the barrier to
> explicit awareness of phonemes. (page 87)

This 'now undoubted need to teach children about phonemes and grapheme–phoneme correspondence' (page 94) arises because children don't teach themselves these things spontaneously, even when placed in the most facilitating circumstances:

> ...explicit awareness of phonemes is not a natural
> development at all: it is... a product of being taught to read.
> (page 87)

Learning to read is, according to Gough and Hillinger (1980), 'an unnatural act'. Teachers need to help children, through direct instruction, to surmount the phonemic barrier.

So, if the teacher has the five roles of facilitator, model, manager, assessor and instructor, what exactly are the implications of this in practice? In relation to the first four roles, Fisher summarises a great body of recent work on practical classroom teaching but, even before discussing the roles, she emphasises the personal qualities of the teacher. She maintains:

> ...the effectiveness of the individual teacher is a crucial
> element in the progress made by the child... Perhaps more
> important than the programme or method used is the
> relationship between the child and teacher and the
> confidence of the teacher in the methods employed.
> (page 50)

The effective teacher gives a high priority to literacy and provides a wide variety of literary experiences for the children. We will now look at each of the roles in turn.

THE TEACHER AS FACILITATOR

Fisher distinguishes two sides to this role. There is the creation of the supportive learning environment and there is the quality of the teacher–child relationship. The creation of the right classroom environment may involve the selection, use and presentation of reading materials, the use made of other available adults, and the relevance and purposefulness of the literacy activities going on – for example, a reading corner including not only a variety of books but also catalogues, telephone directories, comics, brochures and so on, links reading not only with school but with the children's wider experience of written language. Similarly, it is beneficial to set aside a writing area equipped with a variety of different writing materials. Play areas can also be used for literacy purposes by appropriate provision of role-play materials – for example, by setting up a post office, library or travel agent's. The classroom itself, with environmental print, labels, signs and word-processed children's work, can provide yet more practical demonstrations of the uses of literacy.

Next there is the question of the nature and quality of adult-child interaction. These interactions may be with the teacher, non-teaching assistants or parent-helpers. Among the more useful things adults can promote, through talking with children about their reading, are the notions that the purpose of reading is to derive meaning from print and that the reader ought to reflect on and have opinions about what she reads. The readiness of the teacher to share enjoyment, to listen with interest and to ask facilitating and open questions is valuable both in developing the child's sense of what comprehension means and in creating a positive, motivated attitude towards reading.

THE TEACHER AS MODEL

In many ways the teacher as model is an extension of the teacher as facilitator. The teacher's interest in, and speculative questioning about, the stories the child is reading demonstrates the kind of interrogation of the text that it is hoped the child will develop. Vera Southgate *et al.* (1981) observed that simply hearing reading was rarely used instructionally, and more progress was made where teachers placed *less* emphasis on this, but rather spent time talking to the children about the books that they had read. Adams (1990) reports similar findings from America. Quality discussion of the story provides a model of how to comprehend and if this leads to a re-reading of the story to check and savour the meaning, so much the better. Clay (1991) recommends re-reading in order to establish fluency and fuller comprehension.

A further part of the teacher's role as model is to demonstrate reading. She can do this using 'big books', reading to and with the children, pointing to the words as she goes. In so doing she is not only able to demonstrate directionality and discuss word-attack skills, but will also discuss and question the ongoing story with the children. Any story-telling time is an occasion for exploring attitudes and implications together, demonstrating that stories are to be thought about and evaluated. Of course, the teacher also demonstrates reading by reading herself during those quiet reading times Southgate et al. (1981) recommend – times given such names as ERIC (Everybody Reading In Class), DEAR (Drop Everything And Read), SQUIRT (Sh! Quiet, It's Reading Time) and USSR (Uninterrupted Sustained Silent Reading). The teacher provides opportunities both for interaction and imitation in her role as model.

THE TEACHER AS MANAGER

So all-embracing is the concept of the teacher as manager that there is only space here to highlight a few points. Making and using time effectively is essential. Key teaching and learning opportunities occur where the teacher is able to meet the child at the point she has reached, take her hand, as it were, and lead her forward. This is the famous concept of 'the Zone of Proximal Development' (ZPD), derived from Lev Vygotsky (1962). There are things the child can do by herself, there are things she cannot yet do at all, and between them both, there are the things she can do with adult guidance and prompting. Such adult assistance helps her to internalise the procedures and make them her own – 'No, don't tell me. I think I can read it now.' Good management involves matching the instruction to the child's needs and to be able to do this, the teacher-manager needs to know 'where the child is at'. This means keeping track of progress through assessment and record keeping, subjects to be dealt with under a later heading.

Realistically, the teacher cannot manage everything. Much of the child's reading work will be going on without the teacher, as indeed it should be. Using other available adults and engaging the co-operation of parents is invaluable. But a little advice to such helpers on how to listen to, and assist reading will be useful, for example, finger-pointing, giving the child time to work things out, discussing the story and so on.

THE TEACHER AS ASSESSOR

Record keeping is a requirement both of the law and of 'good practice'. It should not simply consist of knowing where a child is at in the reading scheme, but knowing where the child is at in terms of reading skills and strategies.

Miscue analysis, and the approach to listening to reading that miscue analysis encourages, will contribute to the kind of diagnostic information that cumulative reading records require, and also provide the basis for formative assessment, which enables the teacher to plan future activities and instruction appropriately. Such assessment will include listening to children read diagnostically and assessing their comprehension of what they have read. With younger children, attention should also be given to assessing fundamental skills such as directionality, purposeful eye-control and letter knowledge.

The quality of ongoing assessment is vital. Teachers need to be tuned in to continuous individual change. Marie Clay (1991) remarks:

> We begin to produce our reading failures by allowing some children to build ineffective processing strategies which limit what they can do throughout their school careers.
> (page 313)

Her Reading Recovery Programme demands the early identification of problems, and it behoves all teachers to be alert in their diagnostic assessment, especially to no-hope strategies.

THE TEACHER AS INSTRUCTOR

The teacher's job is to ensure learning takes place. Sometimes this means providing experiences, sometimes organising activities, sometimes leading discussion and prompting explorations and, sometimes, it means transmitting information, giving direct instruction in procedures and requiring children to learn things by rote. Different aspects of teaching reading require different approaches, depending to some extent upon how 'natural' or 'unnatural' each of them is. We shall follow them through according to the general formula: phonological skills, graphophonics (including learning the alphabet), syntax and semantics/comprehension. However, this is not an order for them to be taught. As Marilyn Jager Adams (1990) says:

> ...the parts of the reading system must grow together. They must grow to one another and from one another. (page 6)

The parts that need to grow together under strategic control include a wide range of skills: phonological and phonemic awareness; recoding and chunking skills; anticipatory, cross-referencing and self-correcting behaviours, involving the meshing of different strategies; and comprehension, not only for overall understanding, but also to act as a feedback mechanism for checking word identification.

PHONOLOGICAL SKILLS

Phonological processes include alertness to intrasyllabic units and the sounds in words, together with other factors relevant to reading development. For example, listening comprehension is a phonological skill, dependent as it is on short-term auditory memory. Ideally, work in all these areas should start in the home or in nursery school. All these areas can be developed through everyday speaking and listening activities well before reading begins.

Training in phonological awareness among pre-readers and early readers has beneficial effects upon reading development. So what are teachers to do to promote and train children in phonological awareness? Below we look at some of the important areas to be covered.

NURSERY RHYMES

Among pre-readers the obvious place to start is with nursery rhymes, listening to them and learning them off by heart. The teacher can also draw attention to the rhythm, syllables, alliteration and rhymes by clapping in time to the rhythm and talking about the sounds and characteristics of the words, for example, noting that Jack and Jill both begin with the same sound and the same letter, and that Jill and hill end with the same letter pattern. Such activities not only highlight word sounds but also introduce the idea that writing is a phonological code.

LISTENING ACTIVITIES

Listening activities can be used to develop auditory attention and memory. Most basically of all, listening to stories, discussing and recounting them, helps develop attention and interrogative comprehension. Oral listing games can foster (and help you assess) auditory discrimination, memory and sequencing. Children can make up rhyming and alliterating phrases or verses orally, for example, 'I am a frog, and I live in ...?' or 'Matthew likes Mars bars, Gemma likes jam.' Listing games can use alliteration, for example, 'One wet wellie, two tambourines', or 'The parson's cat is soft and sleepy, fluffy and furry...' Children can collect objects for an alliteration or rhyme table, for example, paper, pencil, paint and so on. Games can be invented involving pairing up 'rhyming' pictures, for example, a hat and a cat go together, but not a hat and a coat. Rhyme games can include things like 'I'm thinking of part of my face that rhymes with "rose". Put your finger on your own...'. 'I-Spy' can, of course, be played using either alliteration or rhymes. Exploring the sounds and spellings of children's own names can give them a sense of ownership of such sound-spelling connections.

SOUND SEGMENTATION SKILLS

The beginnings of segmentation can be developed orally through games like 'The Magic Bridge' where the password for getting safely across is to say the initial sound of your name, for example, 'My name is Daniel. D-d-d-Daniel. D-d-d', or 'I am B-Big B-Billy Goat Gruff. B-b-b'. More sophisticated games can be played with words themselves to draw attention to their *sounds* as distinct from their meanings, for example, 'Take the /m/ away from 'mice', and what do you get?' or 'Add a /p/ to 'ill' and what do you get?' Given a model of how to do this, pre-reading children can blend phonemes orally: /m/, /a/, /t/ → mat. Perhaps a little more sophisticated still are 'odd one out' games. Choosing the odd word out from a list of three or four words makes demands both on phonological memory and comparison. For example:

◆ initial sound (alliteration) – 'pig, pet, hen, pie'
◆ rhyme – 'hen, ten, sit, pen'.

GRAPHOPHONICS

DIRECTIONALITY

The child has to learn: where to start (top left, left-hand page); to read left-to-right along the line, processing the letters left-to-right in each word; not to continue across to the right-hand page, but to flick back to the left-hand end of the next line down, and so on. This is best learned by watching the procedure being demonstrated by the teacher, finger-pointing while reading and when writing. Finger-pointing helps the child when reading *and* helps the teacher monitor directionality. Early writing is a powerful influence in establishing the routine but, as with everything else in writing, it behoves the teacher to watch carefully to make sure the child is learning the desired, and not some other, habits!

THE ALPHABET

Effective reading depends fundamentally on instantaneous letter recognition. There are a number of different aspects involved in learning the alphabet:

✦ Learning visual discrimination so as to recognise the significant distinctions between letters, including orientation (for example, distinguishing between 'u' and 'n', 'p' and 'q', 'b' and 'd'). Learning the equivalence between upper and lower case letters, for example, A/a, B/b, as well as the easier C/c, and so on. Similarly, learning the equivalence between the hand-written 'ɑ' and the type-font 'a'.

✦ Learning the names of the letters – necessary for learning the equivalence between the upper and lower case forms (see above and the discussion in Chapter 5).

✦ Learning the sound-values of the letters, including their variations, especially with regard to vowels.

✦ Learning digraphs (for example, 'sh', 'th') and 'context sensitive' rules (for example, 'When two vowels go walking, the first does the talking').

✦ Learning alphabetical order.

While learning alphabetical order is not relevant to initial reading development, the easiest and earliest way to gain familiarity with the names of the letters is to learn to sing the alphabet. Relating this knowledge to a wall-frieze alphabet is a relatively painless way of learning the letters – the task is to relate names to shapes.

Learning the spelling of her own name is a good way to spark off a child's interest in identifying and forming letters. Time spent looking at print and finding the letters she knows encourages attention to letters. Talking about and comparing letter shapes, identifying them by feel in a feely bag, stroking them, modelling them, writing them in the air and on paper while naming them, all reinforce the individual identity of each letter as a visual, kinaesthetic, tactile and phonological unity.

From very early on children should start to learn the relationship between capitals and lower-case letters. Clearly there is scope for confusion here when it comes to writing (but does it matter?), and it increases the immediate learning load. On the other hand, so much environmental print is in capitals, that *not* to teach them early cuts children off from potential learning experiences. After all, they are coming across initial capitals in their own names right from the beginning. A wall-frieze with both upper and lower case letters is a good idea for ready reference and though, as the teacher, you may concentrate on lower-case first, children will incidentally start to pick up equivalences.

GRAPHOPHONIC LEARNING

Graphophonics is about spelling–sound correspondences. The key to effective decoding is the development of orthographic recognition units – that is, recognising spelling chunks as pronounceable units, whether they are whole words like *the* and *other*, or sub-word units like *-ing*, *-ee-* and *inter-*. Learning to read by chunking the printed letters is attained through a variety of routes:

✦ developing the logographic discrimination net through alphabetic learning and early writing in order to establish greater discrimination in terms of perceiving the letters and letter order;

✦ analogical inference, starting with rimes and onsets but developing into onset + vowel and vowel digraph alertness;

✦ the unconscious learning of frequent spelling sequences, and their relationships with pronunciations;

✦ the recognition of syllable units in polysyllabic words;

✦ the learning of morphological units like -ation, inter- and -ing.

✦ synthetic phonics word-attack skills applied to infrequent and unknown words.

Some of these routes have to be deliberately taught (for example, synthetic phonics, morphological analysis) and the others can be facilitated by appropriate teaching approaches. Clearly, phonological development, directionality and alphabetic knowledge are essential prerequisites. The teacher raises graphophonic alertness by:

✦ developing phonemic awareness with the assistance of movable letters, showing how words can be composed and decomposed, and how blending works;

✦ raising awareness of letters, sounds and letter patterns in words generally, and in particular in known words, for example, by collecting rhyming words, words that alliterate, and so on, hunting for known letters or words in a text, hunting for words beginning with a particular letter in a text, looking at initial sounds, final sounds, salient spelling features, and so on;

✦ drawing explicit attention to spelling–sound patterns by helping children discover rime and onset sound relationships, for example, through using rime and onset cards, movable plastic letters, and so on, for exploring word families based on common rimes or onsets (hen, pen, men; sing, sad, sorry, and so on);

✦ using movable letters to show how one word can be transformed into another, how onsets and rimes can remain unchanged while the word is transformed;

✦ looking for known syllables in polysyllabic words, for example, *cat* in 'catkin', but not in 'catch';

✦ segmenting words into morphemes, for example, looking for letter sequences like *-ed*, *-ing*, *-tion*; looking at compound words, for example, postman → postcard; postman → milkman;

✦ sounding out words using synthetic phonics, which builds on letter-sound knowledge, sequencing and blending skills. (Easy success in this will tend to follow writing experience.)

INVENTED SPELLING AND EARLY INDEPENDENT WRITING

The infant teacher who says, 'Just spell it the way it sounds. I'll be able to read it,' gives her children a head start. Her children may produce more spelling mistakes at first, but they will write about three times as much. What is more, within a matter of months, they will do better on spelling tests and will be better at reading. This strategy also develops self-confidence and curiosity about print. Children with initial low reading readiness seem to benefit particularly.

The process of inventing spellings is essentially a process of phonics. In the first instance, however, the child tends to confuse the name of the letter and the sound of the letter so that, for example, the child may produce 'r' to mean either 'are' or 'our'. Such confusions may occur within words such as 'nis' (nice) and 'plas' (place), where the vowel gives its name-sound. Consonant clusters can cause problems and nasals are sometimes lost as in 'wot' (won't) and 'plat' (plant) as a result of problems with auditory (phonemic) discrimination: the 'o' in 'wot' gives its name-sound, but the missing 'n' is presumably not even heard − just as it isn't in the word 'environment' by the many graduates who pronounce and spell it 'enviroment'!

Inventing spelling phonically, where the child is thinking about letter–sound relationships and their sequences, promotes thoughtful and active (even if not accurate) efforts to spell, as with the spelling 'craen' for 'crying'. It seems that it is this attention to letter sequencing that makes the invented speller not only better than the traditionally taught child at spelling infrequent regularly spelled words but also at noticing and learning the spelling of frequent irregular words. Attention given to each letter in sequence helps the child to develop models of the serial probability of letter combinations, an essential aspect of orthographic processing. Promoting invented spelling, then, is a valuable complement to instruction in reading as well as writing, but its effectiveness and value will be greatly enhanced by direct instruction in word analysis and parallel development of consonant blending.

The kind of attention developed by the invented speller to spelling sequences alerts her to spelling 'chunks' (for example, blends, digraphs, rimes), acceptable letter sequences and to spellings in new words she meets. Such attention to spelling greatly enhances reading performance, and this is why experimenting with sound–symbol relationships in writing is to be encouraged. Invented spelling is helpful because it directs attention to the letter-by-letter sequencing of sounds in words. As a result of noticing spellings, children will come spontaneously to want to get spellings right. Inventing spellings is a self-teaching strategy.

SYNTACTIC AWARENESS

Syntactic awareness is one of the most powerful top-down constraints on word and word-sense identification. Marie Clay (1991) observes that 79 per cent of five-year-olds' substitution miscues in reading are syntactically acceptable. So long as the grammar is not too complex, young children seem to be very syntactically aware without any special help. Such awareness depends upon the word-string being held in the short-term auditory memory, and any problems are likely to be related to either short-term memory or sophistication of syntax. Of course, to grow in reading sophistication, children still need to meet variety in syntax, and therefore their experience should not be artificially restricted in this area.

Listening to stories and thereby learning the language of story develops children's syntactic awareness. Oral and written cloze procedures can be used to highlight syntactic awareness and, at a later stage, games involving jumbled sentences and making up sentences to fit a given pattern can draw children's attention to syntactic patterns. For example, children can be asked to invent more sentences to fit the pattern:

The hungry girl   ate   her sandwiches.

Exchanging parts between the sentences can throw up entertaining possibilities, for example:

The dirty car   ate   her sandwiches.

'Her sandwiches? Whose? Its sandwiches?' And so on. In this kind of way, using children's perception of what makes sense, issues about agreement, pronoun reference, subject, verb, object, adjectives and nouns can come under conscious scrutiny without one ever needing to use the terms. Of course, at some stage it might be appropriate to do so, but an exploratory approach places children's intuitive knowledge in the driving seat. Syntactic awareness is, in the first instance, a matter of becoming more aware of what you already know. The best way to develop syntactic awareness is to question and play with language, using grammatical intuition and sense as touchstones.

SEMANTICS AND COMPREHENSION

Ultimately, comprehension is what reading is all about. It depends on both fluency in reading and listening comprehension. So a lot of valuable work in developing reading comprehension can be done in terms of listening comprehension. Both depend on processing language in the short-term auditory memory and the transformation of sentence and discourse meanings, explicit and inferred, into schematic memories.

The quality of teacher–child/children discussion of stories is crucial. Comprehension depends, among other things, on the active application of the children's existing knowledge, so *preview discussion* of a story's theme and setting is useful – 'This story is about tigers. Who knows about tigers?' Such discussion both raises curiosity and anticipation, and activates and adds to the prior knowledge on which understanding depends.

It may be that *during* the story you will want to stop to check whether the children understand some point, whether they are making the necessary inferences, how far they are following the development of the theme and narrative and whether they are anticipating appropriately the way the story is developing. What you are trying to promote is *an ongoing active interrogation of the story*, interpreting events and motives appropriately so as to lead to a focused desire to know what happens next.

When the story is finished, *reviewing* it can help to make it cohere as a meaningful schema. Discussion of events, and inferences about what and why, are one part of such a review. The other important aspect is response – the children's opinions and feelings about characters and events, relating them to their own experiences, are all part of the larger integration of the story into their own schemes of knowledge and values.

Summarising or retelling the story shows how far children can sequence and see the logic of the events, and reconstruct the story schema. It also helps them to get the story straight for themselves and to savour it. With younger children, dramatising the story can also be a useful way of allowing them to explore the events and characters. In listening to or reading the story a second or third time, there is a different kind of anticipation and interrogation in savouring the pattern, sequence, causation, characters, experiences and motives involved, maybe drawing out more inferences and connections than were appreciated the first time round.

The pattern, then, is preview, interrogate, review, and this pattern is also appropriate for children reading on their own. Discussing the reading book the child is working on is often time better spent than listening to the child reading. This is carried out with the intention that the child will internalise these procedures for herself. A well-written story can be trusted to guide the more capable reader appropriately without outside help but, generally, review discussion is useful, even if just to share enjoyment. Teacher and child can meet in a specially rewarding way in a good story.

SUMMARY

The teacher's role in the teaching of reading involves instruction and intervention as well as providing facilitative support and encouragement. Although children are spontaneous problem-solvers, with a drive to learn and make sense of their world as it is significant to them, they still need instruction in things that do not come spontaneously, direction when their strategies are unproductive or have no future mileage in them, and motivation to feel the unnatural act of reading is significant to them. The teacher's role, consequently, involves both proactive and reactive elements. It is a complex and subtle role. To fulfil it, the teacher crucially needs both a theoretical understanding model of the development of the reading process and a diagnostic sensitivity to the child's developing reading strategies. With them both, the teacher will be equipped to teach with the grain of the child's spontaneous development.

REFERENCES

Adams, M.J. (1990) *Beginning to Read: Thinking and Learning about Print* MIT Press.

Ahlberg, A. (1984) *Please Mrs. Butler*, Puffin.

Anderson, E. (1992) *Reading the Changes*, Open University.

Arnold, H. (1982) *Listening to Children Reading*, Hodder & Stoughton.

Arnold, H. (1986) 'Hearing Children Read' from Cashdan, A. (Ed.) *Literacy Teaching and Learning Language Skills*, Basil Blackwell.

BBC (1992) (video) *Teaching Reading*.

Beard, R. (1987, 1990) *Developing Reading, 3–13*, Hodder & Stoughton.

Beard, R. (Ed.) (1993) *Teaching Literacy: Balancing Perspectives*, Hodder & Stoughton.

Bettelheim, B. and Zelan, K. (1991) *On Learning to Read*, Penguin.

Brady, S. and Shankweiller, D. (Eds.) (1991) *Phonological Processes in Literacy*, Laurence Erlbaum Associates.

Brooks, G., Gorman, T., Kendal, L. and Tate, A. (1992) *What Teachers in Training are Taught about Reading*, NFER Nelson.

Bruner, J. and Haste, H. (Eds.) (1987) *Making Sense*, Methuen.

Bryant, P. (1993) 'Phonological aspects of learning to read' in Beard, R. *Teaching Literacy: Balancing Perspectives*, Hodder & Stoughton.

Bryant, P. and Bradley, L. (1985) *Children's Reading Problems*, Basil Blackwell.

Carter, R. (Ed.) (1990) *Knowledge about Language and the Curriculum*, Hodder & Stoughton.

Cashdan, A. (Ed.) (1986) *Literacy: Teaching and Learning Language Skills*, Basil Blackwell.

Chall, J.S. (1983) *Learning to Read: The Great Debate* (revised edition), McGraw Hill.

Chukovsky, K. (1963) *From Two to Five*, University of California Press.

Clark, M.M. (Ed.) (1985) *New Directions in the Study of Reading*, Falmer Press.

Clark, M.M. (1976) *Young Fluent Readers*, Heinemann.

Clay, M.M. (1972, 1979) *Reading: The Patterning of Complex Behaviour*, Heinemann.

Clay, M.M. (1991) *Becoming Literate: The Construction of Inner Control*, Heinemann.

Cox, B. (1989) *English for Ages 5 to 16* ('The Cox Report'), National Curriculum Council.

Donaldson, M. (1978) *Children's Minds*, Fontana.

Donaldson, M. and Reid, J. (1985) 'Language Skills and Reading: a Developmental Perspective' in Clark, M. (Ed.) *New Directions in the Study of Reading*, Falmer Press.

Downing, J. (1979) *Reading and Reasoning*, Chambers.

Ehri, L.C. (1991) 'The Development of Reading and Spelling in Children: An Overview' in Snowling, M. and Thomson, M. (Eds.) *Dyslexia: Integrating Theory and Practice*, Whurr.

Ehri, L.C. (1992) 'Reconceptualising Sight Word Reading' in Gough, P.B. *et al.* (Eds.) *Reading Acquisition*, Lawrence Erlbaum Associates.

Ellis, N. (1991) 'Spelling and Sound in Learning to Read' in Snowling, M. and Thomson, M. (Eds.) *Dyslexia: Integrating Theory and Practice*, Whurr.

Feldman, C.F. (1987) 'Thought from Language: the Linguistic Construction of Cognitive Representations' in Bruner, J. and Haste, H. (Eds.) *Making Sense*, Methuen.

Fisher, R. (1992) *Early Literacy and the Teacher*, Hodder & Stoughton.

Frith, U. (1985) 'Developmental Dyslexia' in Patterson, K.E. *et al.* (Eds.) *Surface Dyslexia*, Lawrence Erlbaum Associates.

Garfield, A. (1992) *Teach Your Child to Read*, Vermilion.

Gollasch, F.V. (Ed.) (1982) *Language and Literacy: The Selected Writings of Kenneth S.*

Goodman Volume 1, Routledge and Kegan Paul.

Goodman, K. (1967) 'Reading: A Psycholinguistic Guessing Game' in Gollasch, F.V. (Ed.) (1982) *Language and Literacy: The Selected Writings of Kenneth S. Goodman Volume 1*, Routledge and Kegan Paul.

Goodman, K. (1973) 'Miscues: Windows on the Reading Process' in Gollasch, F.V. (Ed.) (1982) *Language and Literacy: The Selected Writings of Kenneth S. Goodman Volume 1*, Routledge and Kegan Paul.

Goodman, K. (1993) *Phonics Phacts*, Scholastic Canada.

Goodman, Y. (1990) 'The Development of Initial Literacy' in Carter, R. (Ed.) *Knowledge about Language and the Curriculum*, Hodder & Stoughton.

Goswami, U. and Bryant, P. (1990) *Phonological Skills and Learning to Read*, Lawrence Erlbaum Associates.

Goswami, U. and Bryant, P. (1992) 'Rhyme Analogy and Children's Reading' in Gough, P.B. *et al.* (Eds.) *Reading Acquisition*, Lawrence Erlbaum Associates.

Goswami, U. (1991) 'Recent Work on Reading and Spelling Development' in Snowling, M. and Thomson, M. (Eds.) *Dyslexia: Integrating Theory and Practice*, Whurr.

Goswami, U. (1993) 'Orthographic Analogies and Reading Development' in *The Psychologist*, July 1993, p 312ff.

Goswami, U. (1994) 'Towards an Interactive Analogy Model of Reading Development: Decoding Vowel Graphemes in Beginning Reading' – to appear in *The Journal of Experimental Child Psychology*.

Gough, P.B., Ehri, L.C., and Treiman, R. (Eds.) (1992) *Reading Acquisition*, Lawrence Erlbaum Associates.

Gough, P.B. and Hillinger, M.L. 'Learning to Read: An Unnatural Act', *Bulletin of the Orton Society*, 30, pp 179-96.

Gough, P. B., Juel, C. and Griffith, P.L. (1992) 'Reading, Spelling and the Orthographic Cipher' in Gough, P.B., *et al.* (Eds.) *Reading Acquisition*, Lawrence Erlbaum Associates.

Greene, J. (1986) *Language Understanding: A Cognitive Approach*, Open University.

HMI (1990) *The Teaching and Learning of Reading in Primary Schools*, DES.

Halliday, M.A.K. (1975) *Learning How to Mean: Explorations in the Development of Language*, Edward Arnold.

Harris, M. and Coltheart, M. (1986) *Language Processing in Children and Adults*, Routledge and Kegan Paul.

Hayes, J.R. (1970) *Cognition and the Development of Language*, Wiley.

Juel, C. and Roper Schneider, D. (1985) 'The Influence of Basal Readers on First Grade Reading' in *Reading Research Quarterly* 20, p 134ff, discussed in Adams, M.J. (1990), p 275ff, MIT.

Karmiloff-Smith, A. (1984) 'Children's Problem Solving' in Lamb, M.E. *et al.* (Eds.) *Advances in Developmental Psychology Volume 3* Lawrence Erlbaum Associates.

Lamb, M.E., Brown, A.L. and Rogoff, B. (Eds.) (1984) *Advances in Developmental Psychology Volume 3*, Lawrence Erlbaum Associates.

Language in Action (1974) Macmillan Educational.

Lewis, C.S. (1965) *The Voyage of the Dawn Treader*, Penguin.

Link-up (1973) Holmes McDougall.

Mackinnon, G.E. and Waller, T.G. (Eds.) (1981) *Reading Research: Advances in Theory and Practice Volume 3*, Academic Press.

McNally, J. and Murray, W. (1968) *Key Words to Literacy*, Schoolmaster Publishing.

Marsh, G., Friedman, M.P., Welch, V. and Desberg, P. (1981) 'A Cognitive-Developmental Approach to Reading Acquisition' in Mackinnon, G.E. and Waller, T.G. (Eds.) *Reading Research: Advances in Theory and Practice Volume 3*, Academic Press.

Meek, M. (1982) *Learning to Read*, Bodley Head.

Morais, J. (1991) 'Metaphonic Abilities and Literacy' in Snowling, M. and Thomson, M. (Eds.) *Dyslexia: Integrating Theory and Practice*, Whurr.

Morris, J.M. (1984) 'Focus on Phonics' in *Reading* (1984), 18 (1), pp 13–24, UKRA.

Oakhill, J. and Garnham, A. (1988) *Becoming a Skilled Reader*, Basil Blackwell.

Oxford Reading Tree Teacher's Guide 1 (1986) Oxford University Press.

Patterson, K.E., Marshall, J.C. and Coltheart, M. (Eds.) (1985) *Surface Dyslexia*, Lawrence Erlbaum Associates.

Patterson, K.E. and Morton, J. (1985) 'From orthography to phonology: an attempt at an old interpretation' in Patterson, K.E. *et al.* (Eds.) *Surface Dyslexia*, Lawrence Erlbaum Associates.

Perera, K. (1984) *Children's Writing and Reading: Analysing Classroom Language*, Basil Blackwell.

Perera, K. (1993) 'The 'Good Book': Linguistic Aspects' in Beard, R. *Teaching Literacy: Balancing Perspectives*, Hodder & Stoughton.

Perfetti, C. (1992) 'The Representation Problem in Reading Acquisition' in Gough, P.B. *et al.* (Eds.) *Reading Acquisition*, Lawrence Erlbaum Associates.

Reid, J. (1993) 'Reading and Spoken Language: the Nature of the Links' in Beard, R. *Teaching Literacy: Balancing Perspectives*, Hodder & Stoughton.

Resnick, L.B. and Weaver, P.A. (Eds.) (1979) *Theory and Practice in Early Reading Volume 2*, Lawrence Erlbaum Associates.

Seidenberg, M.S. and McClelland, J.L. (1989) 'A Distributed, Developmental Model of Word Recognition and Naming' in *Psychological Review* 1989, Volume 96, No 4, pp 523–568.

Seymour, P.H.K. and Elder, L. (1985) 'Beginning Reading without Phonology' in *Cognitive Neuropyschology* 1985.

Slobin, D. (1966) 'Grammatical Transformations and Sentence Comprehension in Childhood and Adulthood' in *The Journal of Verbal Learning and Verbal Behaviour* 5, 1966, pp219–227.

Smith, C. (1970) 'An Experimental Approach to Children's Linguistic Competence' in Hayes, J.R. *Cognition and the Development of Language*, Wiley

Smith, F. (1978, 1985) *Reading*, Cambridge University Press.

Smith, F. (1988) *Joining the Literacy Club*, Heinemann.

Snowling, M. (1987) *Dyslexia*, Basil Blackwell.

Snowling, M. and Thomson, M.E. (Eds.) (1991) *Dyslexia: Integrating Theory and Practice*, Whurr.

Southgate, V., Arnold, H. and Johnson, S. (Eds.) (1981) *Extending Beginning Reading*, Heinemann.

Story Chest: Teacher's File (1993) Nelson.

Sunshine Spirals (1993) Heinemann Educational.

Treiman, R. (1992) 'The Role of Intrasyllabic Units in Learning to Read and Spell' in Gough, P.B. *et al.* (Eds.) *Reading Acquisition*, Lawrence Erlbaum Associates.

Treiman, R. and Zukowski, A. (1991) 'Levels of phonological awareness' in Brady, S. and Shankweiller, D. (Eds.) *Phonological Processes in Literacy*, Lawrence Erlbaum Associates.

Tunmer, W.E. and Hoover, W.A. (1992) 'Cognitive and Linguistic Factors in Learning to Read' in Gough, P.B. *et al.* (Eds.) *Reading Acquisition*, Lawrence Erlbaum Associates.

Vygotsky, L.S. (1962) *Thought and Language*, MIT Press.

Waterland, Liz (1988) *Read With Me: An Apprenticeship Approach to Reading*, The Thimble Press.

Weber, R. (1970) 'A Linguistic Analysis of First-grade Reading Errors' *Reading Research Quarterly*, V, 3, pp 427–51

GLOSSARY

(NB Asterisks* indicate where a word is referenced elsewhere in the glossary.)

Active sentences: sentences where the grammatical subject is the 'doer' of the verb-action. (Contrast passive sentences*.)

Alphabetic method: the traditional method of teaching reading by 'see-ay-tee spells cat' routines. (Compare with phonics*.)

Alphabetic principle: where the writing system, comprising letters and combinations of letters, represents the constituent sounds (and not the meanings) of words.

Alphabetic reading: reading by recoding* letters to sounds – effectively the same as phonic reading.

Anaphoric pronouns: pronouns that refer back to nouns previously mentioned within a text*.

Apprenticeship: a term popularised by Liz Waterland to denote one-to-one reading and enjoyment of books between an adult and a child, where the child can take over and relinquish the task of reading as she wishes.

Auditory memory: the short-term working memory* based on the retention of sound-images of words.

Blending: the smooth running together of individual sounds in pronunciation, often referring in particular to consonant sounds, as in bl- and -nd.

Bottom-up processes: interpreting the visual information from the page in order to identify words. (Compare with top-down processes*.)

Cipher: means virtually the same as code*, but is preferred by some writers as being more specific. Thus, cipher reading effectively means alphabetic decoding*.

Cloze procedure: a way of testing contextual comprehension by systematically leaving blank about 10 per cent of words in a continuous passage and asking the reader to fill them in.

Code: a code is a system of representation that depends on conventions, not likenesses. Writing is a code representing the (sounds of the) words of the language. (See also decoding* and recoding*.)

Code-centred approaches: approaches to teaching reading that concentrate on decoding*.

Cognitive skills: skills related to knowing and thinking.

Cohesion: the textual means by which meanings are linked from sentence to sentence through a discourse*, often through the use of anaphoric pronouns*.

Consonant: the letters and letter sounds that aren't vowels*.

Context: the surrounding situation as it influences interpretations of meaning. This term has a wide range of reference, covering things from the immediate subject matter or the grammar of the sentence to general knowledge about what is likely in the world.

Cues: the specific stimuli or clues that children use to help them identify a written word. These cues may be graphophonic*, syntactic* or semantic*. (See also miscues*.)

Decoding: translating print into words.

Digraphs: pairs of letters that operate like a single letter to represent a single sound, for example th, ee, sh.

Directionality: scanning along the direction of the text, left-to-right across, and top-to-bottom down the page.

Discourse: passages of language considered as communication.

Dyslexia: developmental dyslexia is a chronic reading impairment resulting from a phonological* deficit.

Ellipsis: the omission from a sentence of words needed to complete the construction in full, but where the meaning can still be understood. For example: Do you always need to finish a sentence? No, you don't always...

Fixation: when the eye is stationary for a moment, looking at something.

Flashcards: cards with single words on them for rote teaching word recognition.

Formative assessment: assessment aimed at finding out what needs to be taught next.

Fovea: the central and most sensitive part of the retina* of the eye.

Grammar: the rules for putting words together and modifying them in relation to each other to make meaningful phrases and sentences. (See also syntax* and morphology*.)

Grapheme: the written equivalent of a phoneme*.

Grapho-phonemics: the relationships between graphemes* and phonemes*.

Graphophonics: the relationships between spelling patterns and sound patterns in language.

Homographs: words that are spelled the same but mean different things.

Homophones: words that sound the same but mean different things.

Indicative sentences: sentences that make statements rather than ask questions or issue commands.

Inflections: the add-on endings to verbs indicating tense and number, and to nouns indicating plurals, and so on.

Interactive models: models* that explain things in terms of the way top-down* and bottom-up* processes mutually influence each other and contribute to meaning.

Intrasyllabic units: onsets* and rimes*, the two sub-units composing syllables*.

Language experience approaches: approaches to teaching reading that see reading within the context of the child's whole experience of language. The emphasis falls on motivation and the use of context* to establish meaning, rather than upon decoding*. (See whole language approaches*.)

Logographic reading: the rote-learning process of identifying words from arbitrary partial cues. (Contrast with alphabetic* reading which translates the letters into sounds to identify words, and orthographic* reading which identifies words from their spellings.)

Look-and-say: teaching whole words to establish an initial sight vocabulary for reading, often with use of flashcard*.

Miscue: a mistake in word-identification in reading, resulting from incomplete processing.

Morphology: the study of the structure of words in terms of parts (morphemes) carrying specific elements of meaning. In relation to grammar, morphology refers to the way inflections* are used to establish meanings and agreements within a sentence.

Model: a pictorial way of considering a theory as a working structure.

'New phonics': denotes recent approaches to reading based on theories about the importance of phonology in learning to read.

Onset: the part of a syllable* that precedes the vowel* sound.

Orthographic: to do with spellings.

Passive sentences: where the grammatical subject is not the 'doer' but the 'done-to'.

Phoneme: the smallest sound segment that can affect meanings in words.

Phonics: the relationship between the sounds and writing system of a language. It is also a method of teaching reading by encouraging children to sound out the letters and blend* the sounds together, as in 'cuh-a-tuh spells cat'.

Phonological: to do with sounds in words as they relate to meaning. Hence phonological awareness = alertness to constituent sounds in words; phonological conversion = translating printed words into sound words.

Phrasal verbs: verbs composed of a stem* and a preposition*, which have a different meaning from the meaning of the stem, for example, to get on = to advance in a career.

Pragmatics: to do with meanings in specific situations.

Predicate: the part of a sentence that follows the subject, including the verb, object(s) and adverbial(s).

Prediction: the process of anticipating from the preceding meaning what word comes next in a sentence.

Prepositions: function words like *on*, *at*, *to*, that typically precede nouns to indicate time, place, direction and so on.

Priming: effects that predispose the reader to perceiving particular words by reducing the threshold of consciousness.

Psycholinguistic: to do with the psychology of language knowledge. Hence 'psycholinguistic guessing game' = processes of prediction*.

'Real books': non-reading scheme books. This term also relates to an approach to teaching reading that focuses on sharing experiences of quality books and meaning rather than on teaching decoding* techniques.

Recoding: translating print into sound words.

Retina: the sheet of nerve endings at the back of the eye that converts light images focused on it into nerve impulses for transmission to the brain.

Rime: the intrasyllabic unit* consisting of the vowel* sound and any subsequent consonant* sounds in a syllable*.

Saccade: the movement of the eye from fixation* to fixation.

Schema: a mental construction or concept.

Segment: a constituent sound element in a word, for example, a phoneme*, intrasyllabic unit* or syllable*.

Segmentation: identifying segments or constituent parts of the sounds of words.

Self-teaching mechanisms: strategies* that have the effect of enabling the child to learn spontaneously in a self-directed manner.

Semantics: to do with meanings.

Sight vocabulary: words identified virtually instantly on sight. Sometimes used to indicate logographic reading*, sometimes orthographic* reading. Reader beware!

Stem: the core part of a verb to which inflections* or endings may be added as the grammar requires, for example, *add* in 'added'.

Strategy: reading strategy = the manner of tackling a written word to try to make sense of it; teaching strategy = a tactic by which a teacher tries to influence learning.

Syllable: a word segment* consisting of a vowel* sound together with the consonant* sounds that are attached to it, whether preceding or following the vowel.

Syllabary: in the writing system of some languages the characters represent complete syllables*. Such languages have a syllabary rather than an alphabet.

Syntax: the aspect of grammar concerned with word order.

Synthetic phonics: traditional phonics* involving the synthesis of a word by blending* the letter sounds.

Text: the visible writing that embodies a discourse*.

Threshold of consciousness: the psychological notion of a level of stimulus at which the individual becomes aware of it.

Top-down processes: the application of existing conceptual knowledge in making sense of text.

Vowel: the sounds represented by the letters *a, e, i, o, u* and sometimes *y*, and their combinations, which are at the core of every syllable*.

Whole language approaches: the American equivalent of language experience approaches*, strongly opposed to decoding* approaches.

Working memory: the short-term memory in which we sort out our immediate perceptions.

INDEX